A DISCOURSE ON THE METHOD

RENÉ DESCARTES was born at La Haye near Tours on 31 March 1596. He was educated at the Jesuit Collège de la Flèche in Anjou, and at the University of Poitiers, where he took a Licenciate in Law in 1616. Two years later he entered the army of Prince Maurice of Nassau in Holland, and met a local schoolmaster, Isaac Beeckman, who fostered his interest in mathematics and physics. After further travels in Europe he settled in Paris in 1625, and came into contact with scientists, theologians, and philosophers in the circle of the Minim friar Marin Mersenne. At the end of 1628 Descartes left for Holland, which he made his home until 1648; he devoted himself to carrying forward the mathematical, scientific, and philosophical work he had begun in Paris. When he learned of the condemnation of Galileo for heresy in 1633, he abandoned his plans to publish a treatise on physics, and under pressure from his friends consented to have the *Discourse on the Method* printed, with three accompanying essays on topics in which he had made discoveries. In 1641 his *Meditations* appeared, setting out the metaphysical underpinnings of his physical theories; these were accompanied by objections written by contemporary philosophers, and Descartes's replies to them. His writings provoked controversy in both France and Holland, where his scientific ideas were banned in one university; his works, however (including the *Principles of Philosophy* of 1644) continued to be published, and to bring him notoriety and renown. In 1648 he accepted an invitation from Queen Christina of Sweden to settle in Stockholm; it was there he died of pneumonia on 11 February 1650.

IAN MACLEAN is Professor of Renaissance Studies at the University of Oxford and a Senior Research Fellow of All Souls College. Among his publications are *The Renaissance Notion of Woman* (1980, frequently reprinted), *Meaning and Interpretation in the Renaissance: The Case of Law* (1992), *Montaigne philosophe* (1996), *Logic, Signs and Nature in the Renaissance: The Case of Learned Medicine* (2001), and an edition of Cardano's *De libris propriis* (2004).

OXFORD WORLD'S CLASSICS

*For over 100 years Oxford World's Classics have brought
readers closer to the world's great literature. Now with over 700
titles—from the 4,000-year-old myths of Mesopotamia to the
twentieth century's greatest novels—the series makes available
lesser-known as well as celebrated writing.*

*The pocket-sized hardbacks of the early years contained
introductions by Virginia Woolf, T. S. Eliot, Graham Greene,
and other literary figures which enriched the experience of reading.
Today the series is recognized for its fine scholarship and
reliability in texts that span world literature, drama and poetry,
religion, philosophy and politics. Each edition includes perceptive
commentary and essential background information to meet the
changing needs of readers.*

OXFORD WORLD'S CLASSICS

RENÉ DESCARTES

A Discourse on the Method of Correctly Conducting One's Reason and Seeking Truth in the Sciences

Translated with an Introduction and Notes by
IAN MACLEAN

OXFORD
UNIVERSITY PRESS

OXFORD
UNIVERSITY PRESS

Great Clarendon Street, Oxford OX2 6DP

Oxford University Press is a department of the University of Oxford.
It furthers the University's objective of excellence in research, scholarship,
and education by publishing worldwide in

Oxford New York

Auckland Cape Town Dar es Salaam Hong Kong Karachi
Kuala Lumpur Madrid Melbourne Mexico City Nairobi
New Delhi Shanghai Taipei Toronto

With offices in

Argentina Austria Brazil Chile Czech Republic France Greece
Guatemala Hungary Italy Japan Poland Portugal Singapore
South Korea Switzerland Thailand Turkey Ukraine Vietnam

Oxford is a registered trade mark of Oxford University Press
in the UK and in certain other countries

Published in the United States
by Oxford University Press Inc., New York

First published as an Oxford World's Classic paperback 2006

British Library Cataloguing in Publication Data

Data available

Library of Congress Cataloging in Publication Data

Descartes, René, 1596–1650.
[Discours de la méthode. English]
A discourse on the method of correctly conducting one's reason and
seeking truth in the sciences / René Descartes ; translated with an
introduction and notes by Ian Maclean.
  p. cm. — (Oxford world's classics)
Includes bibliographical references and index.
1. Methodology. 2. Science—Methodology. I. Maclean, Ian. II. Title.
III. Oxford world's classics (Oxford University Press)
  B1848.E5M33 2006   194—dc22   2005019297

Typeset in Ehrhardt
by RefineCatch Limited, Bungay, Suffolk
Printed in Great Britain by
Clays Ltd, St. Ives plc., Suffolk

ISBN 0–19–282514–3   978–0–19–282514–8

1

CONTENTS

ACKNOWLEDGEMENTS

I should like to record my gratitude for the kind assistance I received from the following colleagues and friends: Robin Briggs, John Cottingham, Dan Garber, Noel Malcolm, Michael Moriarty, and Richard Parish. I am also very grateful for the support and encouragement I received from Judith Luna of Oxford University Press.

INTRODUCTION

The publication in 1637 of an anonymous book in French entitled *A Discourse on the Method of Correctly Conducting One's Reason and Seeking Truth in the Sciences* marks one of the pivotal moments of Western European thought; it was the work of a formidably clever, radical, rigorous thinker, who in this short, informally presented introduction to his work threatened the very foundations of many prevailing philosophical beliefs, and set an agenda for enquiry into man and nature whose effects have lasted up to the present day. In this introduction to his thought, Descartes set out his novel philosophical and 'scientific'[1] programme, and prepared his contemporaries to receive it, even though they would be looking at it through the prism of their intellectual expectations, which (for the learned among them) had been formed in the traditional framework of Aristotelian philosophy and its characteristic modes of debate. It is, of course, impossible fully to re-create the sense of reading a work for the first time, especially one written so long ago, and in so different a cultural climate; as Bernard Williams pointed out in 1978, we can play seventeenth-century music from seventeenth-century scores on seventeenth-century instruments, but we will hear it with twentieth-century ears.[2] But even though any attempt at reconstruction will be a *pis aller*, I shall nonetheless adopt a historical rather than timelessly philosophical approach to the text, and seek to place it in contexts

---

[1] I shall use 'science' and 'scientific' in this introduction to designate what Descartes would have known as 'natural philosophy', that is, the pursuit of causal knowledge in the investigation of nature. While it is generally agreed that the map of disciplines was very different in Descartes's time from what it is now, there has been much recent debate as to whether a continuity can be perceived from the natural philosophy of the seventeenth century to modern science; by the use of inverted commas, I intend to signal a potential anachronism, but not to take a side in this debate, for an account of which see *Early Science and Medicine*, 5 (2000). The numbers in brackets throughout the Introduction refer to volume and page in the standard edition of the complete works of Descartes by Charles Adam and Paul Tannery, 11 vols. (Paris, 1996): hereafter referred to as AT in the text and notes.

[2] *Descartes: The Project of Pure Enquiry* (Harmondsworth, 1978), 9.

which reveal something of its early impact. I have not attempted comprehensively to cover the whole range of meanings which have been attributed to the *Discourse*; my aim is to set it in the context of the life of its author, to give some inkling of what Descartes himself was setting out to achieve by its publication, to indicate how he came to put its various components together and make it available to the public, and to suggest what its first readers might have made of it.

A Philosopher's Life

René Descartes was born on 31 March 1596 at a village called La Haye in the French province of Poitou (a token of his posthumous prestige was its renaming as La Haye-Descartes in 1793; since 1967 his birthplace has been known just as Descartes). His father was a magistrate in Brittany; through his profession he possessed the status of nobility, being a member of the so-called 'noblesse de robe'. This class was resented by the old military nobility (the 'noblesse d'épée'), who looked on lawyers as little more than pen-pushers; but those who enjoyed the status set great store by it. They were not above inflating their claims to aristocracy by acquiring lands which conferred on them titles ('terres nobles'), and even putting on military airs; such was the case with the otherwise admirably unpretentious Michel de Montaigne (1533–92: a figure important to Descartes in more than one way, as we shall see), whose grand-parents were merchants, whose father was an army officer, and yet who felt able to boast that he was the 'scion of a race famous for its military valour'. On both sides of his family, René's forebears had been doctors and lawyers, prosperous enough to acquire 'terres nobles' for members of their families. René's title, which he used until his mid-twenties, was du Perron: he was known by this title by his Dutch acquaintances in the early 1620s. The sense of status which this background gave him was a motivating force in his later life.[3]

---

[3] See Ellery Schalk, *From Valor to Pedigree: Ideas of Nobility in France in the Sixteenth and Seventeenth Centuries* (Princeton, 1986); Montaigne, *Essais*, ed. Pierre

As Descartes tells us himself, he was a sickly, pale-complexioned child, who suffered from a dry cough (AT 4. 220–1); he was brought up in his grandmother's house, his father being absent in Brittany, having remarried in 1600. In 1607 he was sent away from home to be educated, to the newly founded Collège de la Flèche; this was a Jesuit school, which like others of its kind was established to serve the needs of the professional classes and nobility, as well as to produce Jesuit priests and missionaries. Its second principal, Father Étienne Charlet (1570–1652), was related to Descartes's mother's family. Perhaps through this connection, and because of his delicate constitution, a concession was made: René was allowed to get up later in the morning than the other pupils, a practice to which he adhered for much of his life (in contrast to the ascetic and exacting regime of contemporary scholars, who often rose in the early hours, worked by feeble candlelight, and ruined both their eyesight and health in the process).

The Collège had an impressive and rigorous curriculum, which included the university arts course (the so-called trivium of grammar, logic, and rhetoric, and quadrivium of arithmetic, geometry, music, and astronomy), which was taught as a preparation for degrees in the higher faculties of theology, law, and medicine. This curriculum had been codified and published by the Jesuits in 1599, in its *Ratio studiorum*: it integrated what are now known as the humanities (classical literature, history, drama, and so forth) with scholastic philosophy and theology. The *Ratio* had all of the benefits and all of the defects of such codifications; while it set high standards, it also discouraged innovation, especially in the investigation of natural philosophy. Descartes provided an account of the curriculum in the *Discourse*: he was given a thorough grounding in ancient languages and literatures, grammar, logic, and rhetoric, and instructed in scholastic natural philosophy, mathematics, metaphysics, and ethics. Descartes reacted very differently to these two components. On the one hand, he commented adversely on the logic and philosophy

Villey (Paris, 1965), 2. 11, p. 427: 'la fortune m'a faict naistre d'une race fameuse en preud'homie'; for use of the title du Perron, see Isaac Beeckman, *Journal 1604 à 1634*, ed. Cornelis de Waard, 4 vols. (The Hague, 1939–53).

he was taught, with its rebarbative vocabulary, inelegant syntax, and old-fashioned forms of writing and learning (disputations and 'quaestiones'), although it should be pointed out that he did not entirely lose his taste for it: one or other of St Thomas Aquinas's two voluminous theological *Summas* was a book he took with him—another being the Bible—when he moved to Holland from Paris in the late 1620s. On the other hand, the strong emphasis on humanistic learning and elegance of expression was to turn him into a stylish and fluent writer of Latin. Jesuit schools have long been associated with the claim: 'give me the child, and I will give you the man.' In the atmosphere of Counter-Reformation Europe, it might well be thought that this would entail the inculcation of an intransigent religious outlook founded on unswerving obedience to the Roman Church. There is clear evidence, as we shall see, that Descartes was very reluctant to be seen to oppose this body, even when he secretly believed it was wrong, as in the case of the condemnation of Galileo. In this, he may even have kept in his mind the stricture to be found in the *Spiritual Exercises* of the founder of the Jesuit order, St Ignatius Loyola (1491?–1556): 'to be right in everything, we ought always to hold that the white which I see, is black, if the Hierarchical Church so decides it.' He may indeed have heeded this advice over matters of 'science', but he seems not to have taken from his schooling a personal hostility to Protestants; many became his friends and 'scientific' colleagues, and he himself chose to settle in a Protestant country characterized by the relatively tolerant co-existence there of various religious groups.[4]

Descartes stayed at the school until 1615; he then went on to the University of Poitiers, where, in 1616, he took a Licentiate in Law (a higher degree, academically very nearly the equivalent of the

---

[4] See Stephen Gaukroger, *Descartes: An Intellectual Biography* (Oxford, 1995), 38–61 (there are many biographies of Descartes, which all share a great deal of the same material; this one is very well documented); AT 2. 630 (reference to the Bible and the *Summa*); St Ignatius Loyola, *Ejercitios espirituales*, cuarta semana, 13a regla, in *Obras completas* (Madrid, 1963), 272: 'debemos siempre tener, para en todo acertar, que lo blanco que yo veo, creer que es negro, si la Iglesia hierárchia assi lo determiná'; on Descartes's strong reservations about disputations, see the preface to the French edition of the *Principes*, AT 9B. 7–8. On Descartes's view of the Netherlands as a place of 'such total liberty', see AT 1. 204.

doctorate). This was no doubt at the behest of his father, who might have hoped that he would follow him in his profession. He may also have studied medicine in these years; he appears at some stage to have acquired some skill in dissection. He did not, however, take up the law, but instead went to Holland in 1618, where he joined the army of the Protestant Prince Maurice of Nassau. It is not known what role he fulfilled in the armies to which he was attached: his biographer Adrien Baillet (1649–1701) suggests it was that of engineer, involved with military architecture and fortifications, but he might equally have undergone a form of training as a gentleman soldier. This was not a surprising choice of career for a member of the minor nobility (nor was it unusual to join armies representing confessional interests other than one's own, providing that there was no clash of national interest); throughout his life Descartes was to remain conscious of his status as a gentleman, and some of his attitudes to scholarship and publishing are tinged with an aristocratic disdain for trade. Through his inheritance from his mother, who had died in 1597, he eventually acquired an annual income. This was assessed by one of his early biographers at about 6,000–7,000 livres: a modest sum, but sufficient to ensure independent living, provided that one avoided too many extravagances. Descartes seems to have been naturally frugal; he did not maintain a large retinue, ate and drank in great moderation, dressed in a sober fashion, and avoided socializing—to which, in any case, he was little drawn: on 5 May 1631 he confided to his friend Jean-Louis Guez de Balzac (1594–1654), in a letter (AT 1. 203), that in Amsterdam he paid no more attention to the people he met than he would to the trees on his friend's estate and the animals that browsed there. There is no indication that he suffered financial difficulties until the last few years of his life. Baillet suggests that he was actually richer in the late 1640s than ever before, but his behaviour seems to indicate the reverse; he speaks in letters for the first time of being willing to accept patronage (to Hector-Pierre Chanut, 1 November 1646, AT 4. 535), something which he had steadfastly refused to contemplate up to then.

While in Breda in 1618 he met a schoolmaster and mathematician, Isaac Beeckman (1588–1637), who was to be one of the formative influences on his intellectual development. Until 1628 he was in fairly regular contact with Beeckman; a significant cooling of their exchanges then occurred, due to Descartes's accusation that Beeckman had been boasting about what Descartes had learned from him, which led to the ungracious demand that the musical treatise he had given to Beeckman as a present be returned. Although there was a rapprochement, they never were as close friends again. This was not the only time that Descartes was to fall out with close associates, only later to be partially reconciled with them. One of his biographers refers to the years 1618–19 as Descartes's 'apprenticeship with Beeckman'; in fact, Beeckman was not as good a mathematician as Descartes, but was more up-to-date with practical problems in mechanics, and better instructed in natural philosophy. They discussed (often with Beeckman supplying the question and Descartes the answer) the nature of matter, mechanics, hydrostatics, optics, acoustics, and gravitation; from these exchanges Descartes composed his first work, a short treatise on music entitled *Compendium musicae*, which was completed in December 1618 and presented to Beeckman.[5]

In the meantime, Descartes had left the army of Maurice of Nassau and had joined that of the Catholic Elector Maximilian, duke of Bavaria, in Germany, where he was present at the coronation of the Holy Roman Emperor Ferdinand II at Frankfurt in September 1619. Later in that year he found himself in winter quarters, near Ulm according to some, or Neuburg according to others;[6] and on 10 November (as Baillet tells us), shut up in a stove-heated room, he experienced three dreams which profoundly influenced the course of his life. He refers to these visions obliquely in the *Discourse*; but the details of the dreams were known only after his early papers were circulated posthumously (AT 10. 173–257). He had spent the day meditating on the 'foundations of a wonderful science', and it was in the context of this ambitious and all-embracing project that he interpreted his dreams. In the third of these, he was confronted with

[5] Adrien Baillet, *La Vie de Monsieur Descartes* (Paris, 1691) 2.460–1 (on income); Gaukroger, *Descartes*, 65–103, 222–4.

[6] Geneviève Rodis-Lewis, *Descartes: His Life and Thought* (Ithaca and London, 1998), 36.

a pregnant question (a line remembered from the classical writer
Ausonius): 'what road in life shall I follow?' There have been many
attempts to explain the psychological processes revealed by his
account of this event: for some, it expresses a young man's disquiet
about the intellectual presumption implicit in his proposed enquiries
into nature; for others, it is a sign of a nervous breakdown, or even a
bad migraine. It is noteworthy in respect of this early experience that
in his later published writings he never referred to dreams as bearers
of spiritual messages, but considered them as no more than corporeal
in origin and subject to error; but there is one reference in a letter of
November 1646 to 'following one's inner inclinations' (AT 4. 530)
which may suggest that dreams could be taken seriously. If so, the
possibility might also be entertained that the event imbued him with
a sense of a divinely inspired mission; it was his destiny to pursue the
'wonderful science' and reveal it in due course to his contemporaries.
He could not, of course, do this by referring to the heavenly directive
he had received in this numinous way, especially as he was put off by
any whiff of occultism; the current vogue for alchemy and magic,
with its obscure and secretive lore revealed only to initiates, repelled
him (AT 1. 40, 10. 374). So the works he eventually published scru-
pulously exclude any reference to mysteries and to knowledge available only to initiates, and rigorously eschew all mental activities
except those which could be ascribed to a thinker exploiting the
natural light of his reason.[7]

Inspired by this vision, but also by work he had already begun, he
composed over the next decade a work which was published posthumously with the title *Rules For the Direction of Our Native Intelligence* (*Regulae ad directionem ingenii*); this confirms that from an early
date he was interested in formulating a general method for 'scientific' enquiry. His movements at this period of his life are difficult to
ascertain. It is not known when he ceased to be a soldier. Baillet tells
us that he returned to France in 1622; it is known that in May of that
year he sold the property through which he held the title du Perron

[7] Baillet, *Vie*, 1. 81; Ausonius, *Eclogarum liber*, 2: 'Quod vitae sectabor iter?';
Les Olympiques de Descartes, ed. Fernand Hallyn (Geneva, 1995); Gaukroger, *Descartes*,
105–11.

with its seigneurial rights; it seems likely that he set out for Italy at some point in 1623, and while there visited the shrine of Our Lady of Loreto, which, according to one early biographer, he had solemnly undertaken to do immediately after his dreams in 1619 (another indication, perhaps, if it is true, that he saw the dreams in terms of a divine directive). By 1625 he was again in Poitou, where he flirted for the last time with the idea of taking up a legal career; he then travelled on to Paris, to remain there until 1628. This was a tense time in the capital: the vogue for allegedly lax morality among young gentlemen, connected with the production of libertine (in part obscene) literary works and publicly expressed indifference (if not worse) to religion, had led to a number of thunderous denunciations of atheism and free-thinking, and the trial of the prominent poet Théophile de Viau (1590–1626). Descartes makes one brief reference to this atmosphere and to the free philosophizing associated with it in a letter to Mersenne dated 6 May 1630 (AT 1. 150), and quotes once in a letter of 1 February 1647 from a poem by Théophile (AT 4. 617); but there is no reason to believe that he ever was beguiled by free-thinking, or to doubt the sincerity with which he upholds his own personal religious belief and his determination to find arguments to refute deists and atheists.[8]

He consorted in Paris with two former pupils of the Collège de la Flèche (although there is no evidence that he knew them while at school): Claude Mydorge (1585–1647), a gentleman of leisure and independent means, who like Descartes devoted himself to 'scientific' problems; and Father Marin Mersenne (1588–1648), a Minim friar, who was already a well-published author on theology and its relation to natural philosophy, an implacable enemy of free-thinkers, and an indefatigable correspondent of the learned community throughout Europe. Until his death in 1648, Mersenne was to remain Descartes's mentor and principal contact in the capital. He came to know other important figures in the 'scientific', literary, and religious communities, including Jean de Silhon (1596–1667), who, like him, was to write as a lay person on the soul; Father Guillaume

---

[8] Gaukroger, *Descartes*, 135–86; Antoine Adam, *Les Libertins au XVIIᵉ siècle* (Paris, 1964).

Gibieuf (1591?–1650), through whom he was later to seek acceptance by the theological community of Paris; the stylist and epistolary writer Jean-Louis Guez de Balzac; a fellow mathematician and physicist, Étienne de Villebressieu (d. 1653); the librarian and antiquary Gabriel Naudé (1600–53); and Jean-Baptiste Morin (1583–1656), whose broad range of interests included astrology. In these circles he quickly obtained a reputation as a powerful and original thinker; during his association with them, he discovered the sine law of refraction in optics (which had been independently discovered by other mathematicians at about this time, and is now known as Snel's Law), and came to learn of Mersenne's interest in mechanics and his mathematical approach to nature. He would also have heard discussed some of the most innovative modern thinkers, such as Francis Bacon (1561–1626), whose *New Organon, or True Directions For the Interpretation of Nature* (*Novum organum, sive indicia vera de interpretatione naturae*) had appeared in 1620. He pursued the question of the certainty of mathematics, in order to warrant its use as a guiding discipline in physics; this seems to have led to disappointment on the one hand, and, on the other, a desire to extend the project of finding certainty into a much broader field (a desire encouraged by the influential Counter-Reformation cleric Cardinal Pierre de Bérulle (1575–1629), who had been present at a meeting at which Descartes powerfully refuted a proponent of chemical philosophy, and was impressed by him). By late 1628 he put into execution his plan to retire from Parisian intellectual life, stimulating though it was, and live in the Netherlands, which was to be his home (with frequent changes of address) for the next twenty years. It was there, in 1634, that he entered into a relationship with a maidservant known only to posterity by her first name, Helena; she had a daughter by him, born on 19 July 1635, whom he recognized as his. The child's death in 1640 seems to have caused much distress to Descartes. He also entered into contact with the Dutch diplomat and polymath Constantijn Huygens (1596–1687), who was to help him in his relations with the Dutch court.[9]

The broader project on which Descartes set to work (sometimes

---

[9] On all the friends and contacts mentioned above, see Gaukroger, *Descartes*, 471–80.

referred to by his correspondents as his 'Physics') was given by him the title *The Universe* (*Le Monde*), and was to be an ambitious account of the physical world on mechanistic principles. Most of two parts of this work survived (the *Treatise on Light* and the *Treatise on Man*), and were found among his papers after his death; the third part, on the soul, was not found, and may not have been written. At the same time, we learn from a letter which Guez de Balzac wrote to him on 30 March 1628 (AT 1. 570) that he was planning an auto-biographical essay entitled 'the story of my mind' (*L'Histoire de mon esprit*). He also had by this time sketched out a set of metaphysical and epistemological essays which were transformed into the *Medita-tions* of 1641. But disaster was to strike. *The Universe* was predicated on a Copernican cosmology, which had already been censored by the Inquisitors of the Roman Church in 1616; seventeen years later it was officially and very publicly condemned in the same body's judgement on Galileo's *Dialogue Concerning the Two Chief World Systems*. Descartes immediately abandoned his plans to publish *The Universe*. He had never been very keen on the idea of publication, not only for the snobbish reasons suggested above—that it smacked of trade—but also because he was very protective of his privacy: as a token of this, his adopted motto was the adage of Ovid, *bene qui latuit, bene vixit* (he who remains well hidden, lives well: AT 1. 286). His Parisian friends pressed him, however, to make his philosophy known, and succeeded in inducing him to compose the *Discourse on the Method of Correctly Conducting One's Reason and Seeking Truth in the Sciences*, and to set down his achievements in optics, meteorology, and geometry. These works appeared in French in 1637; they included an invitation to the learned world to respond to them by sending critiques to Descartes's publisher, who would forward them to the author for consideration and reply. He declared himself keen to engage in discussion this way, rather than in public disputation, because he believed that the latter mode of debate encouraged parti-cipants to win at any cost, rather than pursue the truth for its own sake (AT 9B. 8–9). In fact, the suggestion did not bear fruit as he may have hoped in this case, although it did a few years later in the case of the *Meditations*, which were published with objections and replies.

Having once embarked on the career of author, Descartes saw

himself obliged to continue, if only to avoid misrepresentation by others (something about which he was very sensitive). In 1641 the *Meditations on First Philosophy, Together With the First Six Sets of Objections with Replies* appeared in Latin; a second, enlarged, volume came out a year later, and a French translation by the duc de Luynes, to which Descartes gave his approval, followed in 1647. The *Meditations*, whose first-person singular is not so much the historical Descartes as it is any reflective person working their way through a set of arguments, do not describe philosophical discoveries, but present them in the order in which readers are enjoined to enact the process of discovery for themselves. In this they are unlike the *Discourse*, which is presented as a personal and historical narrative. In 1644 his Latin *Principles of Philosophy* followed; three of its four books are about 'science' (physics and natural philosophy) rather than strictly philosophical principles. It was published in French in 1647 in a translation by Abbé Claude Picot (1601?–68), a Parisian priest who was converted to Descartes's philosophy by the *Meditations*, and who came as a friend to look after Descartes's financial affairs in the last years of his life. Also in 1644 a Latin version of the *Discourse* appeared, which made this text accessible to the wider learned community. Other writings followed, often in response to criticisms of his work, for by the early 1640s Descartes had become notorious throughout Europe; these included the *Comments on a Certain Broadsheet* (*Notae in programma quoddam*), which appeared in 1647. Descartes's philosophy (or rather, a version of it which he disowned) had been enthusiastically adopted by his disciple Henrick de Roy (Regius) (1598–1679), of the University of Utrecht; the rector of that same Calvinist establishment, Gijsbert Voet (1588–1676), had it condemned there in 1641. Regius was the author of the broadsheet which provoked the *Comments* of 1647, in which he set out a version of Cartesianism unacceptable to Descartes, who very much resented being drawn into such controversies; he looked upon them as distractions from his true vocation, which was to develop his system in order eventually to provide a secure grounding for ethics and medicine. He himself had also hoped that his philosophy might be adopted by the Jesuits for use in their colleges; but as he ruefully told Huygens in a letter dated 31 January 1642 (AT 3. 523), he found as many opponents in their midst as he did among the Protestants of the Low Countries.[10]

The last work to appear in his lifetime, in 1649, was the *Passions of the Soul* (*Les Passions de l'âme*), written, like the *Discourse*, in French. This may well have been inspired by his contacts, beginning in 1642, with Princess Elizabeth (1618–80), the Calvinist granddaughter of James I and daughter of the deposed king of Bohemia, who was living in exile in The Hague; in her correspondence with him, she had pressed him to explain the interaction of soul and body in his system. He had already made explicit his decision to write accessibly, not only for members of the court but also for women; her lucid and shrewd questioning must have confirmed for him the wisdom of this decision.

By 1647 the financial stability which had allowed Descartes to live independently and to reject all offers of patronage seems to have been threatened. In that year he returned to Paris, to arrange to take up the royal pension that he had been granted in that year—an expensive procedure, involving the outlay of money to obtain a royal warrant before any pension was received. The following year saw the beginning of the civil wars in France known as the Fronde, which effectively put an end to royal patronage for half a decade (in spite of Baillet's claim to the contrary, it seems that Descartes was never to receive a penny of royal largesse). It may have been such material factors that persuaded him to accept the patronage offered by Queen Christina of Sweden (1626–89), who was actively seeking to surround herself with prominent scholars and thinkers. In 1649, having put his affairs in order, he set out with all his papers for Stockholm, dressed, to the astonishment of his acquaintances, in the clothes of a fashionable courtier, with his hair in ringlets.[11] After a rather unsatisfactory beginning to his stay there, during which he made some new French friends and was entrusted with some nugatory tasks, he was eventually summoned to the royal palace on Christina's return to her capital, to instruct her in his philosophy. She ordained that this

---

[10] Gaukroger, *Descartes*, 357–61.

[11] AT 5. 411 has the description of Brasset, the secretary of the French Embassy at The Hague.

should take place from 5 a.m. to mid-morning; the man with the weak chest, who had spent the greater part of his life rising late and nursing his health, was now exposed not only to the rigours of a Stockholm winter in the early hours of the morning, but also to the infectious pneumonia of his friend the French ambassador, Hector-Pierre Chanut (1601–62), in whose residence he lived, and whose bedside he attended during his illness. Descartes in turn contracted pneumonia, and died on 11 February 1650.

Descartes's correspondence, which was published soon after his death, reveals something of the character of its author, as do his early biographers. Baillet, in a somewhat hagiographical account of Descartes's life, describes him as a man with a serene and affable expression, careful in his consumption of food and wine, content to keep his own company, without personal affectations or foppishness (he only took to wearing a wig towards the end of his life, for reasons of health). Baillet assures us that if he was at all vain, this was only a superficial vanity; he was modest, indifferent to public acclaim, and had a gift both for fostering the careers of those for whom he was responsible, and for the friendship of his peers. Among Descartes's modern biographers, only Geneviève Rodis-Lewis has retained many of these features; she has also stressed his frequent changes of address, and attributed them to his overriding desire to be left alone to pursue his search for scientific and philosophical truth. His elusiveness was noted even by his contemporaries: his acquaintance Claude de Saumaise (1588–1653) wrote to a correspondent in 1637 that Descartes kept well away from others ('à l'escart') even in a small town like Leiden, and wittily suggested said that his name ought to be spelt 'D'escartes' (AT 1. 365); Descartes himself wrote on more than one occasion that he disliked having neighbours (AT 1. 203; 3. 616). While conceding that he had a quick temper, Rodis-Lewis also points out that he was often generous with his time, and received even lowly visitors who came to consult him; and in spite of his conviction that animals were no more than machines (AT 6. 56–9), he kept a dog called M. Grat ('Mr Scratch'), of whom he may even have been fond.[12]

---

[12] Baillet, *Vie*, 486–502; Geneviève Rodis-Lewis, *Descartes*.

The adage, 'there is nothing more praiseworthy in a philosopher than a candid acknowledgement of his errors'—advice offered by Descartes to Regius in January 1642 (AT 3. 492)—would flow naturally from the pen of the Descartes described in Baillet's biography; but it has struck others as out of character in a man who seems never to have accepted the correction and critique of others. He never fell out, it is true, with his closest acquaintance Mersenne, although he offended him on occasion, but with many other contemporaries his relationship ran into difficulties arising from his touchiness, his high assessment of his own work, his low assessment of the intelligence of those around him, and his fastidious and self-protective sense of privacy. One modern philosopher-critic has described him as 'lofty, chilly and solitary', cultivating 'a certain reserve and self-sufficiency in life and manner';[13] to these unendearing characteristics others have added arrogance, a contempt for others which was not always justified, and a capacity to bully those he looked upon as inferior in intellect to himself. He instructed the long-suffering Mersenne to treat his adversary Jean de Beaugrand (1595?–1640) with contempt, and described his letters as fit only for use as lavatory paper; the work of Pierre de Fermat (1601–65) was 'dung'; mathematicians who criticized his geometry were said to be 'flies'; and although he invited his contemporaries to criticize the *Discourse* and the works that followed it, those who took up his invitation came in for a great deal of contumely. Gilles Personne de Roberval (1602–75) is said to be 'less than a rational animal'; Pierre Petit (1598–1677), 'a little dog who barks after me in the street'; Thomas Hobbes (1588–1679), 'extremely contemptible' for daring to call his work into question; others who, having criticized him, did not accept his refutation of them, were described as 'silly and weak'.[14] Descartes was also not above mystifying his correspondents, and making fun of them by setting them difficult or incomplete mathematical problems (AT 2. 336); he compounded this with an unwillingness to disclose his work to others (e.g. AT 1. 367–8) which seems almost to make his

---

[13] Williams, *Descartes*, 24.
[14] Gaukroger, *Descartes*, 323, assembles these comments.

attack on alchemists and occult philosophers for their secretiveness hypocritical. Unsurprisingly, he had a low opinion of the vast majority of his readers, confiding to Mersenne that he did not believe them capable of recognizing the truth of his arguments (AT 3. 436). If there is a feature which redeems to some degree such disagreeable attitudes and behaviour, it is Descartes's honesty and integrity. He may have had an exaggerated sense of his own abilities, but (with the possible exception of his snobbery and his silence over his sense of a personal prophetic mission), the account he gives of his thought-processes and his motivations is frank and scrupulous.

Descartes was buried in Stockholm; in 1666 it was decided that his remains should be exhumed and returned to Paris, to rest eventually in the abbey church of Sainte-Geneviève. At the exhumation the French ambassador was allowed to cut off the forefinger of Descartes's right hand, and a captain of the Swedish Guards may well have removed the skull and replaced it with another. This removed skull was then traded several times, before ending up in the hands of the Swedish chemist Jons Jacob Berzelius, who in 1821 offered it to the palaeontologist Georges Cuvier; it is now to be found in the Musée de l'Homme in the Palais de Chaillot in Paris. The body, meanwhile, found its way eventually to the abbey church of Saint-Germain-des-Prés, where it now lies.[15]

This dismemberment is emblematic of the posthumous fortunes of Descartes's work and doctrine, parts of which have been taken up in different ways at different times, even if his philosophical and 'scientific' doctrine was recognized as a coherent system in his lifetime. By 1650 the adjective 'Cartesian' had emerged; it designated principally his mechanistic philosophy. This was opposed not only by Aristotelian traditionalists, but also by other radical thinkers, and was a powerful motor in the debate about the nature of matter and motion, even if none of his physical theories is now looked upon as correct. At the same time, the *Discourse* had another, more diffuse effect. Its radical programme, which did not require philosophical and 'scientific' training but only the employment of 'good sense', appealed to those who had not received a formal education, notably

---

[15] Ibid. 416–17.

women, who felt empowered by his promotion of the image of the well-reasoning individual. By the mid-1650s, in Paris, 'the free use of reason' was associated with various radical views, some of them feminist, and Descartes was seen as its champion and a liberator from prejudice: 'Cartesiomania' broke out. He was also seen as a dangerous radical in another way: his theory of matter posed problems for the Roman Catholic doctrine of transubstantiation (although Descartes insisted that it did not: see AT 2. 564; 3. 349, 543; 4. 163–70); in 1663 his works found their way onto the Roman Inquisition's *Index of Forbidden Books*, in the category of those which needed correction before they could be published: a supremely ironic fate, given Descartes's strenuous efforts not to offend the Church.

Thereafter, Descartes developed into the national emblem of a specifically French kind of rationalism, and was attacked or defended as such in contradistinction to the empirical philosophy of the English. This opposition was fostered by early Enlightenment thinkers such as Montesquieu and Voltaire (to the disadvantage of Descartes). By the time of the French Revolution he had been turned into a representative of republican thought, deserving of a place in the pantheon of such French heroes; in the nineteenth century he came to be seen as a petit-bourgeois Catholic thinker, before being appropriated by the French educational system and made into the model of clarity of thought and good style in French. It is hardly surprising, therefore, that in 1987, on the three-hundred-and-fiftieth anniversary of the publication of the *Discourse*, a book appeared with the title *Descartes c'est la France*.[16]

Across the Channel, meanwhile, in more recent times Descartes, has been heralded as an honorary practitioner of analytical philosophy, even in some ways its founding father; and although his accounts of the relationship of mind and body, or the existence of other minds, or that of possible other worlds are seen as flawed, he has set the agenda for a certain sort of philosophical training, and the standard for rigorous introspective philosophical speculation. His

[16] See Stéphane Van Damme, *Descartes: essai d'histoire culturelle d'une grandeur philosophique* (Paris, 2002); the author of *Descartes c'est la France* is André Glucksman.

more recent biographers have enquired whether his philosophy drives his 'science' or vice versa, whether they are interdependent, and what role his religious belief plays in his thinking. To some degree these are questions of emphasis, and mark the perpetual revisionism to which all historical thinking is prone; they also reveal the complex and many-faceted nature of his work, the interdependence of its many aspects, and its continued ability to provoke even after three and a half centuries.

The Genesis of the Discourse *and its Development*

Descartes never intended to publish a book like the *Discourse*; his plan was to fulfil a promise to his Parisian friends to set down an account of his world system, which would be called *The Universe*. So the *Discourse* and the essays which accompany it are a substitute for something else, which would have been more comprehensive, more coherent, and more 'scientific' in character. The essays which follow the *Discourse* are described by Descartes as no more than 'examples' of his method in action; in a letter to Mersenne written a few months before its publication, he claims that the *Discourse* itself only refers to his method and its coming into being, and does not state it formally anywhere in the text: 'I haven't been able to understand clearly what you object to in the title,' he writes, 'for I am not saying *Treatise on the Method* but *Discourse on the Method*, which means *Preface or Notice on the Method*, to show that I do not intend to teach the method but only to speak about it' (AT 1. 349). This was a matter of disappointment to his Parisian acquaintants, as Jean-Baptiste Morin pointed out in a letter to him dated 22 February 1638; it prevented them from engaging in a direct critique of the principles of Cartesian physics (AT 1. 537–57).

I have already suggested that one might see the dreams which Descartes experienced in 1619 as decisive in forming in him the ambition to discover some new general account of nature; one road which he might have taken to fulfil this was that of assiduous study of all relevant previous authors. He explicitly discards this as a correct strategy in the *Discourse*, not only because he had already been inculcated with what he saw to be unsound ancient philosophy and an unsatisfactory world system (the Aristotelian), but also, as he frequently admits in his writings and his letters, because he found reading the work of others tiresome. His (not very large) library at his death consisted almost entirely of books that had been given to him by his friends; to various of his correspondents he expresses his dislike of 'fat tomes', and asks them to recommend short books on subjects he wishes to study (AT 1. 221, 251; 3. 185; 5. 176–7); an early comment in his unpublished *Private Thoughts* (*Cogitationes privatae*) runs as follows: 'in the case of most books, once we have read a few lines and looked at a few of the diagrams, the entire message is perfectly obvious. The rest is added only to fill up the paper' (AT 10. 214). There is another, more serious, reason to reject the accumulation of the views of others as a road to truth. Descartes does not quote the popular dictum, 'Plato is my friend, Socrates is my friend, but truth is a greater friend' (to which I shall return below), but he alludes to it. 'We shall not become philosophers if we have read all the arguments of Plato and Aristotle, but are unable to form a secure judgement on the matters in hand', he avers in the *Rules For the Direction of Our Native Intelligence* (AT 10. 367). He consistently recommended the 'light of reason' as the best guide; but he was later to recognize the power of philosophical name-dropping, for he gloomily confided to Mersenne on 30 September 1640 that he had decided in future to back up his arguments with the authority of others, as 'truth by itself is so little respected' (AT 3. 184).[17]

Throughout the 1620s Descartes had been working on geometry and optics, although it seems that the final versions of these works (and the meteorological treatise) were not written until 1635. I have already mentioned that he was known to be planning an auto-biographical essay entitled 'the story of my mind' in 1628; Guez de Balzac wrote to him on 30 March of that year that 'it is [eagerly] awaited by all your friends . . . it will be a pleasure . . . to read of the path you have followed, and the progress which you have made, in [discovering] the truth of things' (AT 1. 570–1). It would seem that

---

[17] On these and similar quotations and their currency, see Ian Maclean, *Logic, Signs and Nature in the Renaissance: The Case of Learned Medicine* (Cambridge, 2001), 191–3.

the language of this essay was to be the vernacular; one model for this, which Descartes certainly perused in spite of his aversion to reading in general, is Galileo's controversial *Dialogue Concerning the Two Chief World Systems* of 1632; another was the *Essays* of Montaigne, a writer certainly known to Descartes, but only named once in all his writings (AT 4. 575). Like Descartes, this sixteenth-century author was a legally trained gentleman of leisure, who engaged in a broad range of reflections (including an assessment of his own education) and recorded them in a deliberately informal way; Descartes emulated only Montaigne's project, and consciously rejected his practice of reading widely, excerpting anecdotes and quotations, and musing on his own life and times. Part One of the *Discourse*, written during Descartes's Paris days, may have been adapted from the account of his intellectual formation to which Guez de Balzac refers. Whereas in his correspondence on mathematical and optical subjects Descartes was content to write in either Latin or French, the decision to incorporate his intellectual autobiography in the work of 1637 may have swayed him to write the whole text in the vernacular.

The proof of the existence of self and God, which forms Part Four the *Discourse*, probably dates from the same period or a little later. Descartes mentions a treatise on metaphysics to Mersenne in a letter dated 15 April 1630 (AT 1. 145); this seems to have accompanied the composition of the ambitious account of the universe entitled *Le Monde*, a version of which was begun while Descartes was still in Paris. Mersenne and others repeatedly urged Descartes to complete this work, referred to also as his 'Physics', even as late as April 1637 (AT 1. 367). Details about his progress are given in various letters of the early 1630s. On 5 April 1632 Descartes wrote to Mersenne:

I can tell you that although the treatise which I promised you at Easter is almost finished, I would nevertheless prefer to keep hold of it for a few months, as much to revise and polish it as to supply some necessary diagrams which I am finding a nuisance, for, as you know, I am no draughtsman, and am very slapdash over things from which I myself can learn nothing. If you accuse me of having so often failed to keep my promise to you, my excuse will be that the only thing that has up to now made me defer setting down the little I know has been the hope of learning more and being able to add to the work. For instance, in what I presently have to hand, I did not originally intend, after the general description of the stars, the heavens, and the earth, to give an account of particular bodies on the earth, but only to deal with their various qualities. In place of this, I am now adding something on their *substantial forms*, and trying to show the way to discover them all in time by providing *experiments and observations* to support my arguments. This is what has taken me away from the work these last days, for I have been engaging in various experiments to discover the *essential differences* between oils, ardent spirits or alcohols, ordinary water and acids, salts, etc. (AT 1. 242–3)

As the words italicized here by me show (Descartes also sometimes marks them in this way in letters and texts), Descartes is still relying on the scholastic vocabulary which elsewhere he decries; this letter also reveals him, against the popular image of him as a cerebral rationalist, to be habitually engaged in experiments and observations, a feature of his 'scientific' practice throughout his life. In June 1632 Descartes wrote again to his closest Parisian friend:

I am now here in Deventer; I have decided not to leave here until the *Dioptrics* has been completely finished. For the last month I have been weighing up whether to give an account of how animals are generated in *The Universe*. I have finally decided not to, because it would take me too long. I have finished all that I intended to put in it about inanimate bodies. It only remains for me to add something about the nature of man. (AT 1. 254)

This passage gives us an insight into the confidence Descartes had in his method; he was willing to contemplate producing his own account of animal generation, apparently without reference to the Aristotelian text on the subject, or the more recent work of the Paduan natural philosopher Fabricius ab Aquapendente (1533–1619).[18] Yet more news about progress was forthcoming in late 1632:

I shall discuss man in *The Universe* more than I thought, for I am setting out to explain all his main functions. I have already written up the vital

---

[18] See Andrew Cunningham, 'Fabricius and the "Aristotle Project" in Anatomical Teaching and Research at Padua', in *The Medical Renaissance of the Sixteenth Century*, ed. A. Wear, R. K. French, and Iain M. Lonie (Cambridge, 1985), 195–222.

functions, such as the digestion of food, the pulse, the distribution of nourishment, etc., and the five senses. I am now dissecting the heads of various animals, so that I can explain what imagination, memory, etc., consist in. I have seen the book *De motu cordis* [William Harvey's *On the movement of the heart*] which you spoke to me about some time ago, and I find myself slightly at odds with his opinion, although I only read it after having completed what I had to say on this topic. (AT 1. 263)

From these and other letters, we may infer that by the beginning of 1633 most of the elements which were to compose *The Universe* were in draft form: of the *Discourse*, only Parts Two and Three seem not to have been written out in some form or other. Descartes had made good progress towards satisfying his friends' and admirers' pleas to give a full account of his new philosophy. On 22 July 1633, he wrote again: 'My treatise is almost finished. I still have to correct it and describe it, but because I don't need to find out anything new, I have such difficulty working on it that if I hadn't promised you more than three years ago to send it to you by the end of this year, I don't believe that I could complete it. But I am very keen to keep my promise' (AT 1. 268).

We are able to know what form most of the treatise would have taken, as a manuscript of Part One (on light) and Part Two (on man) survived among Descartes's papers (AT 11. 3–202). The first treatise deals first with perception in general, the nature of heat and light emanating from fire, hardness and liquidity, vacuum and imperceptibles, and the number of the elements, before passing on to the description of the new world imagined by Descartes as the parallel to this one. A chapter follows on the laws imposed by God on nature, which regulate all natural things. Thereafter, accounts are given of the sun, stars, planets, comets, moon, and earth; weight and light are discussed, and tides explained by the movement of the earth. The treatise on man describes the human body as a machine, and investigates the movement of the blood, animal spirits, the senses, hunger and thirst, digestion, and the brain and its functions. The account given by Descartes of the work in Part Five of the *Discourse* is therefore quite faithful, although the omission of the discussion of tides, which depended on the assumption that the earth moves, is to be noted; this is due to Descartes's reaction to the Galileo affair, which caused a crisis in Catholic Europe in the relations between the Church and the 'scientific' community. To assess the effect of this, we shall have to return to the earlier part of the century, to see how Descartes's friend and mentor Mersenne dealt with an earlier manifestation of this crisis, which arose in 1616, and then show the repercussions of the Galileo affair of 1633 in France and Italy.

Galileo, Mersenne, and the Church: Authority and Truth

From the thirteenth century onwards a conflict existed between the Roman Catholic Church (through its bishops, its councils, and its faculties of theology) and philosophy. The introduction of Aristotelianism had highlighted a number of incompatibilities between ancient and Arabic thought and Christian doctrine, over such issues as the nature of the soul (whether material or immaterial, mortal or immortal), the intellect (whether individuated, or shared by all humanity), and the universe (whether eternal, or created *ex nihilo* as in the account of the Book of Genesis). This conflict came to express itself in the opposition of those who rely on written authority (of an institution, or a text such as that of Aristotle or the Bible) and those favouring free philosophical speculation, who adopted such catchphrases as, 'Plato is my friend, Socrates is my friend, but truth is a greater friend', and the ancient satirist Horace's declaration that he was 'not bound over to swear as any master dictates' (*nullius addictus iurare in verba magistri*), which in due course was to become the motto of the Royal Society of London; these dicta, as we shall see, are quoted by Descartes's friend Mersenne, and are referred to by Descartes himself, in connection with the problems faced by them both.[19]

The eminent Italian mathematician, physicist, and astronomer Galileo Galilei (1564–1642) was convinced by 1598 of the truth of the Copernican theory of heliocentrism. In 1609–10 he constructed a telescope for himself, discovered the four moons of Jupiter (which,

[19] See n. 16, above, and AT 3. 796–7 (letter to Huygens, 10 Oct. 1642); 10. 367 (*Regulae*, 3).

according to traditional cosmology, could not have satellites), and perceived that the Milky Way was a collection of stars and the moon was not in fact a perfect sphere (as all celestial bodies were supposed to be), but had an uneven surface like the earth; all of these observations flew in the face of Aristotelian and Ptolemaic cosmology, and were received with great interest throughout Europe, even in Rome, where at the behest of Cardinal Roberto Bellarmino (1542–1621), the Jesuit College confirmed Galileo's findings. Galileo soon attracted to himself a number of enthusiastic supporters, including the Neapolitan Carmelite Paolo Foscarini (1580–1616), who published a letter extolling the new cosmology in 1615. But the fact that the literal sense of parts of the Old Testament was apparently incompatible with Copernican cosmology alarmed the Roman Catholic's Church's Inquisitors; they issued a condemnation of Foscarini's pamphlet, and formally censored part of Copernicus' book.[20]

The Inquisition was a medieval institution; it had been recast by Pope Paul III in 1542 as the Congregation of the Holy Office, and adapted to combat Protestantism, mainly in Italy, although its powers, wielded by six cardinals, extended to the whole Church. Whereas the medieval Inquisition had focused on popular theological misconceptions which resulted in the disturbance of public order, the Holy Office was concerned with orthodoxy of a more academic nature, especially as it appeared in the writings of theologians. In its first years the activities of the Roman Inquisition were relatively modest in scope; but Pope Paul IV expanded these, and in 1554 ordered the Congregation to draw up a list of books which could be deemed to offend faith or morals. This resulted in the first *Index of Forbidden Books* (1559). By the seventeenth century an impressive number of powerful Counter-Reformation figures had been members of the Roman Inquisition; it is generally agreed that they were enlightened and cultured men. For all this, they were responsible in Italy for the imprisonment of innovative thinkers of the stature of Giordano Bruno (1548–1600) and Tommaso

[20] On Galileo, see Stilman Drake, *Galileo at Work: His Scientific Biography* (Chicago, 1978); Richard S. Westfall, *Essays on the Trial of Galileo* (Rome, 1989).

Campanella (1568–1639). Both of these figures published in the vernacular. The Inquisitors were particularly sensitive to books which were accessible to the non-learned public; indeed, they ordered the execution of the former of these heterodox thinkers. They claimed universal jurisdiction, but their *Index*, which underwent constant updating and revision, was not accepted in France. There, secular legal assemblies (the *parlements*) alone had the power of suppressing books, although various bodies (including certain religious orders and the Faculty of Theology of the University of Paris) were able to issue approbations or condemnations of publications. The difference in religious atmosphere between the two Catholic countries is indicated by the fact that Campanella was imprisoned for many years in Italy, and on his release was granted refuge and protection in France by none other than its chief minister (also a cardinal) Armand du Plessis de Richelieu (1585–1642) himself, in the year following the imprisonment of Galileo (1634).[21]

The real target of the Inquisitors in censuring Foscarini in 1616 was Galileo: he was summoned to Rome to answer to them, and instructed to express his views discreetly; after this interview the Inquisitors issued the following text on 5 March of that year, which Mersenne quotes in full in his long commentary on the early chapters of the Book of Genesis (the *Quaestiones celeberrimae in Genesim*) of 1623:

This Holy Congregation has also learned about the spreading and acceptance by many of the false Pythagorean doctrine, altogether contrary to Holy Scripture, that the earth moves and the sun is motionless, which is also taught by Nicolaus Copernicus' *On the Revolutions of the Heavenly Spheres* and by Diego de Zuniga's *On Job*. This may be seen from a certain letter published by a Carmelite Father, the title of which is *Letter of the Reverend Father Paolo Antonio Foscarini, on the Pythagorean and Coperni-*

---

[21] See Michel-Pierre Lerner, *Tommaso Campanella en France au XVIIe siècle* (Naples, 1995). Campanella was, it is true, very well treated in Rome, where he performed astrological services for Pope Urban VIII; indeed, this figure organized his transfer to France as a way of evading a new and embarrassing request by the authorities in Naples, where he had been held in very harsh conditions for many years, that he be sent back to answer further charges there. But this fact does not render the general point about the difference in religious atmosphere in the two countries invalid.

*can Opinion of the Earth's Motion and Sun's Rest and on the New Pythago-
rean World System* . . . In this letter the said Father tries to show that the
above-mentioned doctrine of the sun's rest at the centre of the world and
the earth's motion is consonant with the truth and does not contradict
Holy Scripture. Therefore, in order that this opinion may not spread any
further to the prejudice of Catholic truth, the Congregation has decided
that the books by Nicolaus Copernicus (*On the Revolutions of Spheres*) and
Diego Zuniga (*On Job*) be suspended until corrected; but that the book
of the Carmelite Father Paolo Foscarini be completely prohibited and
condemned; and that all other books which teach the same be likewise
prohibited . . .[22]

Mersenne held strong views both about the authority of this
judgement and the relation of 'scientific' truth to Catholic doctrine.
These he expressed in his commentary on Genesis. In its Preface he
repudiates the view that Catholic doctors and theologians follow
only Aristotle and 'swear by his words', referring to one of the dicta
quoted above; referring to the other, he claims that truth is most
friendly to Catholics of all thinkers, for they are able to readjust their
beliefs in the light of experience and observation. He acknowledges
that there is a problem in how difficult passages of Holy Writ are to
be interpreted (for example, chapter 10 of the Book of Joshua, in
which the sun is said to stand still in the sky: this is the passage on
which Galileo writes the most); he refers here to the principle of
accommodation invoked by St Augustine, according to which the
literal sense of Scripture can be set aside, if it can be shown that the
purpose of the text is to accommodate itself to common human
experience (for example, that the sun rises and sets, and moves
across the sky). Mersenne claimed that as no definitive theological
statement about the meaning of passages which support this way of
perceiving the movement of the heavens had been issued by the
Church, the matter was still to be resolved.[23]

Later in the same work he returned to the issue of error and
heresy, in an article entitled 'whether anyone is able, without at least

---

[22] *Quaestiones celeberrimae in Genesim* (Paris, 1623), col. 904.
[23] Galileo interpreted Joshua 10 in the letter to Grand Duchess Christina of Tuscany,
of 1615: see Galileo, *Opere*, ed. Antonio Favaro (Florence, 1964–6), 5. 309–48;
Mersenne, *Quaestiones in Genesim*, preface.

a mark of heresy or error, or without danger of temerity, to hold and defend the opinion that the earth moves and the heavens are immobile'; it is pertinent to quote at length what he says, because it prefigures very closely the line that Descartes himself was going to take:

First, it must be laid down that heresy is nothing other than pertinacious error in faith, which is located in a refusal to believe what it is agreed that the Church has put forward to be believed . . . I designate as heretics those who pertinaciously, and by an act of the will after due reflection, call into question things which the Church puts forward to be believed even if they do not expressly dissent from them . . . An opinion is called erroneous, if it denies something which, although not itself a matter of faith, nevertheless is able to be deduced as an incontrovertible consequence of a matter of faith: as for example that Christ was capable of laughter, because he was a man, and so forth . . . An opinion should be deemed temerarious, if without any reason it is affirmed contrary to the unanimous consensus of the doctors.

With these points established, it is easy to reach the judgement that the view which attributes motion to the earth and denies it to the heavens is not heretical; nor is it an error in faith, since the Church has not yet put anything on this issue forward to be believed . . . In fact, the Church did not decree that all the details in Holy Writ are to be believed to the point that we instantly ought to give credence to them in the way that they seem to have meaning for us; for the meaning in which we believe is that intended by the Holy Spirit and declared by the Church, else our faith would be contrary to itself, and would change wherever it attributes one sense to one place and a different one to another. But those places of Scripture which deny the motion of the earth or attribute it to the heavens or the stars have not as yet been declared or expounded by the Church in such a way that we ought to believe them in their literal sense, and that they should be understood in a way they literally sound . . . we ought first to listen to the Church, and from her learn whether anything should be taken in its proper sense or metaphorically . . . there are a thousand other places in Scripture, which are not to be expounded according to the literal sense . . . God has willed that Holy Writ accommodates itself to our understanding and senses, especially in those things, which have to do with nature and with things visible. This is clear from the bodily members attributed to God, such as feet, shoulders, ears, eyes, a thigh, and wings. And I do not see why we should not be able to determine whether those places of Scripture which affirm that the earth stands still, where the issue has not been settled by the Church, are to be understood literally . . . there is nothing preventing the passage in which Joshua ordered the sun to stand still upon Gibeon and the moon in the valley of Ajalon being able to accommodate itself to our senses, which deem the stars and the planets to go around daily in their whole course, from rising to setting, since nothing is present which could correct the senses by reason, and establish that the same thing is happening as with those human beings who, when they are being transported on a ship, trust in their senses alone, and believe themselves to be standing still and the harbour to be approaching or receding, or the banks of the river to be moving by. I seem to remember that St Augustine follows the literal sense in interpreting Holy Writ whenever no problem arises with another place in Scripture, or with a decree of the Church, or with reason. But in truth, those who want the earth to be endowed with motion, and on the basis of reason want to deny that it is at rest, if they are Catholics, will be prepared to obey a decree or determination of the Church on this issue, and as her true sons and faithful members, to submit themselves altogether to her.[24]

This is a somewhat tortuous passage, revealing not only embarrassment, but also an implicit suggestion that the Inquisition's judgement was not of sufficient weight to decide the issue in question; Mersenne's references to the Church imply a conciliarist position, which sees the Church in Council as the only legitimate body to determine a point of doctrine. This suggestion would seem to create a space in which pious Catholics could work without showing disobedience to the Church, provided that they were discreet. Such a position was, however, compromised by the events which followed the publication of Galileo's *Dialogue* in 1632. Galileo may well have felt secure in publishing this pro-Copernican work for various reasons, not least that his patron, Matteo Barberini (1568–1644), who in 1624 had indicated that he was sympathetic to Galileo's astronomical views, had just been elected pope as Urban VIII. But the book caused a furore, and its sale was suspended six months after its publication. Galileo was summoned to Rome, where Urban VIII (possibly angered by what he took to be a personal slight in the

---

[24] Mersenne, *Quaestiones in Genesim*, ix. 6, cols. 901–3.

Dialogue) decided in June 1633 that Galileo should be imprisoned for life.[25]

In November 1633, Descartes wrote the following to Mersenne:

I had indeed intended to send you *The Universe* as a New Year gift, and only two weeks ago I was still quite determined to send you at least a part of it, if the whole work could not be copied in time. But I must confess that I recently made enquiries in Leiden and Amsterdam as to whether Galileo's *World System* was not already there, because I seem to remember hearing that it has been published in Italy last year. I was told that it had indeed been published but that all the copies had immediately been burnt at Rome, and that Galileo had been convicted and punished. I was so shocked by this that I almost decided to burn all my papers or at least to let no one see them. For I could not imagine that an Italian such as Galileo, who was also, as I understand it, well looked on by the pope, could have been made a criminal for any other reason than that he tried, as he no doubt did, to establish that the earth moves. I know that some cardinals had censured this view some time ago, but I thought I had heard it said that it was being taught publicly even in Rome. I must admit that if the view is false, so too are the entire foundations of my philosophy, for it can be demonstrated from them quite clearly. And it is so closely allied to every part of my treatise that I could not take it away without making the whole work defective. And as I would not for all the world want any work of mine to contain a single word that could be disapproved of by the Church, I have preferred to suppress it rather than to make it available in a mutilated form. I have never felt any inclination to produce books, and would never have completed this one if I had not been bound by a promise to you and some other of my friends; it was thus my desire to keep my word to you that constrained me all the more to work on it . . . There are already so many views in philosophy which are no more than plausible and which can be maintained in debate that if my views have no greater certainty than that and cannot be approved of without controversy, I refuse ever to publish them. Yet, I would look ungracious if, having promised you the work for so long, I tried to fob you off with a flippant reply of this sort; so, after all, I shall not fail to let you see as soon as I can what I have composed, but I ask you kindly to allow me another year to revise and polish it. . . . I ask you also to tell me what you know about the Galileo affair . . . (AT 1. 270–2)

---

[25] See William Shea, *Galileo in Rome* (Oxford, 2003).

Descartes was further perturbed by an official Catholic document issued in nearby Liège in September 1633, which he reproduces verbatim in a letter to Mersenne:

The said Galileo, therefore, who had confessed at an earlier interrogation, was summoned to the Sacred Tribunal of the Inquisition, interrogated, and detained in prison. As he had done on a previous occasion, he clearly showed himself to be of the same opinion, though he pretended that he put forward his view only hypothetically. The outcome is that after discussing the matter thoroughly, the Most Eminent Cardinals of the Commissionary General of the Inquisition have pronounced and declared that the said Galileo is under strong suspicion of heresy, in so far as he has followed a doctrine which is false and contrary to Holy and Divine Scripture, namely that the sun is the centre of the universe and does not rise or set, and that the earth moves on the other hand, and is not the centre of the universe, insofar as he has been of the opinion that this doctrine could be defended as worthy of belief, even though it has been declared contrary to Holy Scripture. (AT 1. 306)

The reference to Galileo's unsuccessful line of defence—that he was treating Copernicanism not as a true doctrine but a convenient hypothesis for the computation of celestial events—alarmed Descartes most: this had been, since the first publication of the *De revolutionibus* in 1543, the favoured line taken by a number of Catholic and Protestant astronomers to defend their use of Copernican theory, and would have suited his own purposes very well. His next surviving comment is found in a letter to Mersenne of February 1634, and reiterates the view expressed by his Parisian friend in his commentary on Genesis:

The knowledge that I have of your virtuous nature makes me hope that you will think even better of me when you see that I have decided wholly to suppress the treatise I had produced, thereby losing almost all of my work of the last four years in order to give my complete obedience to the Church, since it has condemned the view that the earth moves. Yet, all the same, as I have noted that the condemnation has not yet been ratified by the pope or the Council (it was made by the Congregation of Cardinals set up to censor books), I should be grateful to know what the view on this matter is in France and whether their authority has been sufficient to make the condemnation an article of faith. I have come to the view that the

Jesuits have helped to get Galileo condemned: Father Scheiner's entire book clearly shows that they are no friends of his. Besides, the observations in the book provide so many proofs which remove from the sun the motion attributed to it that I cannot believe that Father Scheiner is not himself privately persuaded of the Copernican position; a thought I find so shocking that I dare not write down my feelings on the matter. (AT 1. 281–2)

The Jesuit Father Christoph Scheiner (1575–1650) of Innsbruck had published a book entitled *Rosa Ursina* between 1626 and 1630, which agreed with Galileo's claims about sunspots but attacked heliocentrism; Descartes seems here most shocked by his supposed hypocrisy, although there is nothing in this or any subsequent writings by Scheiner to suggest he was anything other than sincere in his cosmological beliefs.

It would seem that, up to this point, Descartes's communications with Mersenne were not intended for public consumption; that does not seem to be the case with the letter of April 1634, which begins with a strangely formal (and indeed otiose) opening statement (it is highly likely, in spite of the mysterious non-arrival of part of their correspondence (AT 1. 292), that Mersenne knew about the Galileo affair, and knew also that Descartes knew of it), and repeats points that already had been made in their correspondence: this indicates, I believe, that Descartes wanted the letter to be circulated in the appropriate quarters in Paris as a quasi-public declaration of his position (a practice he refers to in an earlier letter to Mersenne: AT 1. 178):

I am sure that you know that Galileo was recently reprimanded by the Inquisitors of the Faith, and that his views about the movement of the earth were condemned as heretical. Now I must confess to you that all the things I set out to explain in my treatise, which included the doctrine of the movement of the earth, were so interdependent that it is enough to discover that one of them is false to know that all the arguments I was using are unsound. Though I was of the opinion that they were supported by very certain and uncontrovertible proofs, I would not wish, for anything in the world, to maintain them against the authority of the Church. I know that it might be said that not all the decisions of the Roman Inquisitors become immediately articles of faith, but must first be considered by a Council of the Church. But I am not so fond of my own ideas as to want to use such legalistic arguments as a way of clinging on to them ... I desire to live in peace and to continue the life I have begun under the motto 'he who remains well hidden lives well' ...

As for what you tell me of Galileo's experiments and observations, I deny them all; but I do not conclude the motion of the earth to be any less worthy of credence ... (AT 1. 285–6)

The similarity to the attitudes expressed by Mersenne in 1623 quoted above is striking. Descartes then refers to the work of a priest, just possibly Mersenne himself, but more plausibly Ismaël Boulliau (1605–94), who had indicated that he wanted to use Descartes's physical explanations of the heavens, and whose cosmology was Copernican:

I am astonished that a man of the Church should dare to write about the motion of the earth, whatever excuses he may give for doing so. For I have an official document about Galileo's condemnation, printed at Liège on 2 September 1633, which contained the words, 'though he pretended that he was putting forward his view only hypothetically'; they seem thereby to forbid even the use of this hypothesis in astronomy. This prevents me from venturing to let him know any of my thoughts on the topic. Moreover, I do not see that this censure has been endorsed by the pope or a Council of the Church, but only by a specific congregation of the cardinals of the Inquisition: so I do not altogether abandon the hope that the same may happen as with the Antipodes, which were similarly condemned long ago. So in the fullness of time my *Universe* may yet see the light of day; in which case I shall myself need to employ my own arguments ... (AT 1. 288–9)[26]

The reference to the Antipodes, the existence of which had been denied in an eighth-century Church Council, is found also in Mersenne, and was a convenient way of reminding the Roman Church that doctrines it adopted or condemned had varied over time. It is somewhat puzzling that Descartes should have reacted so strongly in this open letter to the Roman condemnation of a doctrine that had not been condemned in Paris; from his retreat in the

[26] The suggestion of Boulliau is made by Adam and Tannery; Robert Lenoble, *Mersenne ou la naissance du méchanisme* (Paris, 1943), 404, suggests that Mersenne is here referred to.

Netherlands he had absolutely nothing to fear from the Inquisition itself, and would have had nothing to fear in the French capital either. One part of the explanation might be that he hoped—a hope he expressed in later correspondence—that his philosophical system would be adopted by Jesuit schools in France, and saw it necessary to set down where he stood on the matter of Copernicanism, as elements of it were presupposed in his new physics. The private and fastidious Descartes may also have shuddered at the thought of being exposed to public shame by being associated with the Parisian free-thinkers of the 1620s, whose alleged atheism he had set out to refute. What emerges from this letter is the claim that Descartes's system is not a hypothesis (this had been outlawed by the Liège letter); it is in fact, as we shall see, the hypothesis of a hypothesis: he has recourse to the fiction that he is describing not the world as it is, nor the phenomena of the world as they can be explained by a mental construction such as heliocentrism, but a fictional history of the coming-into-being of a world which is parallel to this one, but is not this one. His extreme sensitivity to the Galileo condemnation may in part be explained, therefore, in the light of his aspiration to have his world system supplant that of Aristotle in Jesuit and other schools in France.

On 14 August 1634 we have the first record of Descartes's direct encounter with Galileo's book:

Mijnheer Beeckman came here on Saturday evening and lent me the book by Galileo. But he took it away with him to Dordrecht this morning, so I have only had it in my hands for thirty hours. I took the opportunity of leafing through the whole book; and I find that he philosophizes very well on motion, though there is very little he has to say about it that I find completely true . . . In *The Universe* I had also explained [the ebb and flow of the tide] in terms of the motion of the earth, but in a quite different way to his . . . (AT 1. 303–4)

At some point in 1634 Mersenne himself chose publicly to comment on the Galileo affair in two vernacular texts, one entitled *New Questions* (*Questions inouyes*), the other *Theological, Physical, Ethical, and Mathematical Questions* (*Les Questions théologiques, physiques, morales et mathématiques*); he may have been prompted to do this because

Galileo was being discussed in such popular Parisian institutions as the 'Bureau d'Adresse', a forum for open debate run for the delect- ation of curious and non-specialist audiences by Théophraste Renaudot (1584–1653). This Protestant publicist enjoyed the protec- tion of none other than Richelieu himself, who seems to have seen it to be in France's interest to foster a degree of open debate as a way of marking his nation's distance from the papacy. The motion of the earth had been discussed in 1633 in the Bureau d'Adresse; Renau- dot, who was also responsible for a weekly news organ (the *Gazette*) duly reported Galileo's condemnation in it, and translated its text in full; but in a gesture consistent with the ecclesiastically independent policy of his patron, he went on in 1634 to print the previous year's debates about the motion of the earth. For his part, Mersenne pub- lished in his *Theological Questions* another, more accurate, French translation of the whole text of the condemnation, and of Galileo's abjuration; he also returned to the issue of the authority of the text of the Bible and of the Inquisition. After setting out the various positions dispassionately, but not putting up counter-arguments to all of Galileo's points, he recommends obedience to the Church, but discreetly suggests at the same time that the issue has not yet been definitively settled by a formal decision of the Church in Council. In his own accounts of the arguments for and against the earth's motion, it is not difficult to sense his strong sympathy for the Copernican position. He was advised that this did not show suf- ficient submission to the Church, and reissued the *Questions* with a more acceptable text; however, he circulated the first version to trusted correspondents, and ended his consideration with a refer- ence to the Pauline verse about human ignorance (which might well refer also to ecclesiastical blindness too): 'for now we see through a glass, darkly: but then face to face.'[27]

Descartes, meanwhile, continued to tinker with his manuscript.

---

[27] Mersenne, *Questions inouyes* (Paris, 1634), q. 11; *Les Questions théologiques, physiques, morales et mathématiques*, ed. André Pessel (Paris, 1985), qq. 34, 37, 44, 45 (both versions); Howard M. Solomon, *Public Welfare, Science and Propaganda in Seventeenth-Century France: The Innovations of Théophraste Renaudot* (Princeton, 1972); *Premiere centurie des questions traitees ez conferences du Bureau d'Adresse* (Paris, 1635), 65–8; 1 Cor. 13: 12. See also Lenoble, *Mersenne*, 399–400.

The Galileo affair had caused him to suppress the publication in full of his treatises, but he was able (in Part Five of the *Discourse*) to give quite a full résumé of their contents, omitting only any reference to that which would commit him to the view that the earth moved (the chapter on tides—the same caution can be seen to influence Part Three of his *Principles of Philosophy*, published ten years later). Descartes wrote to Mersenne in the late summer of 1635 that he had revised and completed the *Dioptrics*; on 1 November of that year he wrote to Huygens about his plan to publish this treatise as well as the *Meteorology* with a 'preface' (AT 1. 329–30), and he responded in February 1637 to Mersenne's suggestion that the *Discourse* should precede the three treatises, which he eventually adopted. By that time the process of its production had already begun.

The Publication of the Discourse

We have seen that the volume published in June 1637 is an amalgam of various different works, composed over a long period. The idea of a work on geometry (including optics) dates from Descartes's inter-action with Beeckman; the first version of Part One of the *Discourse* dates back to Descartes's Paris days; Part Four was in draft around 1630; the *Dioptrics* was ready in October 1635, a month or so before the *Meteorology*. The final version of the *Geometry* was composed during the printing of the *Meteorology*. The composite work (on which Descartes worked hard to confer a sense of unity) was origin-ally to be called 'The Project of a Universal Science Which Can Bring Our Nature To the Highest Degree of Perfection. With Diop-tics, Meteorology, and Geometry, in Which the Most Curious Matters Which the Author Could Have Chosen To Establish the Universal Science He Is Proposing Are Explained in Such a Way That Even the Unlearned Will Be Able To Understand Them' (AT 1. 339); this was abandoned for the eventual title some time in 1636, probably after consultation with Mersenne.[28]

Descartes moved to Leiden in March of that year; he confided in Mersenne that the most prominent of all Dutch publishing houses,

---

[28] For the dates of composition, see Gaukroger, *Descartes*, 187–320.

the Elzeviers, were rather grandly expecting him to pay court to them (something that his aristocratic nature made him loath to do), so he had decided to look elsewhere for a printer. He considered sending his manuscript to Paris, but doubted whether his handwriting was legible enough or his diagrams well enough drawn to be reliable copy for submission to a compositor; he was also keen on a contract which would give him 200 copies for distribution (AT 1. 338). He entered into an agreement with the Leiden printer-publisher Jean Le Maire (or Maire) on 2 December 1636, which restricted Le Maire to producing two editions totalling no more than 3,000 copies, and gave Descartes the number of presentation copies he desired. This was a hard bargain, for authors did not usually receive as many copies for distribution to their friends and patrons; I do not think, however, that Descartes was impelled by meanness in this case (although there is a certain amount of circumstantial evidence that he was very careful with his money). He had, after all, offered to put up the money to guarantee the publication of a Life of Saint Elizabeth in October 1631, which Mersenne was keen on having printed in Holland (AT 1. 221). His manner of negotiating may well have something to do with his status as a gentleman. By distributing the copies to his colleagues and friends, he was engaging in an aristocratic culture of gift-giving, an important practice of the society to which he belonged and in which he moved. He was also rather loftily disowning an interest in the fate of the rest of the edition; even though he clearly hoped that a broad public would read his work, his personal intention was to communicate his views to the chosen few from among the number of his fellow-scholars and the court. Evidence of this attitude recurs when, in 1640, he discussed with Mersenne the arrangements for publishing the *Meditations*. He had originally only planned to have an initial print-run of about twenty to thirty copies of this work, which he proposed to finance himself, for him to send to the 'most learned among the theologians' (AT 2. 625); it was only when he realized that it would, willy-nilly, be more widely circulated (as recipients would lend their copies to other readers) that he relented, and changed his view (AT 3. 183).

Jean Le Maire (1577?–1657) was a member of the liberal

(remonstrant) wing of the Calvinist Walloon Church; he may not have been as prominent as the Elzeviers, but he was an enlightened, shrewd, enterprising, and long-established publisher. He had taken over the family business in 1603, and his portfolio of authors eventually included a number of important contemporary Dutch and Flemish humanists, including Daniel Heinsius (1580–1655), Justus Lipsius (1547–1606), and Gerard Vossius (1577–1649), as well as the great Erasmus (1469–1536). He also had strong connections with French expatriate scholars such as Claude de Saumaise and André Rivet (1572–1651); he even published works by Descartes's Parisian acquaintances Guez de Balzac and Gabriel Naudé. The period of time the *Discourse* took to print—more than five months—suggests that Descartes was an exacting author. He certainly had very specific requests, including the production of a number of large-paper copies of the *Geometry* to allow their owners to write copious notes in the margins; he claims in a note he appended to the *Discourse* that he had to deal with non-Francophone compositors, which may have compounded the difficulties he experienced in the printing house, but provided him with an excuse for the errors to be found in the text.[29]

There were other problems that emerged along the way, not least that of the 'privilege', or licence to print. This was effective only in a given jurisdiction: Descartes wanted one to be obtained for his work in both France and the Netherlands to protect it against piracy. It seems that his friend Huygens obtained for him the Dutch privilege; Mersenne was entrusted with the task of securing the French one, which he did with characteristic zeal: indeed, too much zeal for the taste of the fastidious Descartes. Royal privileges were expensive things; in order, probably, to ensure that Descartes would have nothing to pay, Mersenne made supplication to the Crown on his behalf

[29] Gustave Cohen, *Ecrivains français en Hollande dans la première moitié du XVIIe siècle* (The Hague and Paris, 1920) (pp. 503–4 for the Descartes privilege); AT 3. 235, 448 (letter to Mersenne of 17 Nov. 1641 about the publication of the *Meditations*, whose printer also contracted to give a very large number of free copies to Descartes; this letter also reveals Descartes's misconceptions, about the economics of publishing); Ronald Breugelmans, *Fac et spera: Joannes Maire, Publisher, Printer and Bookseller in Leiden 1603–57* (Houten, 2003).

in appropriately hyperbolical terms. These were enshrined (as was then the practice) in the preamble to the document, which was signed in the king's name on 3 May 1637:

Given that discovery in the sciences and the arts, accompanied by demonstrations and applications, is a product of superior minds, this has caused princes and states to receive inventors with every sort of gratification, so that their states might become more flourishing as a result of their discoveries. So it is that our well-beloved Descartes made it known to us that by long study he has come across and demonstrated many useful and beautiful things previously unknown in the human sciences, which touch on various arts and the ways of applying them ... (AT 6. 518)

The text continues in the normal way, setting out the names of the works protected by the licence and the legal penalties incurred if it is infringed; even here there are signs of royal favour, for the privilege generously covered all present and future works by Descartes for ten years, and gave him a much better share of any fines levied: whereas normally the Crown took a third share, this is forgone, leaving only two joint beneficiaries, namely, the poor and the author. But Descartes was furious. He was named in the document, whereas he had studiously kept his name off the title-page; this offended his sensitive aristocratic and private nature as much as did the dithyrambic compliments. He allowed only an extract of the privilege to be printed in the *Discourse* (the full text appeared, however, in subsequent publications), and protested to Mersenne, who was understandably hurt after all his efforts to save Descartes money and enhance his prestige; Descartes was later to apologize for his ungenerous reaction.[30]

There is evidence that much, if not all, of the *Discourse* and the accompanying treatises were circulated before publication, in some cases in the form of page proofs. Jean de Beaugrand, an agent for the Chancery in Paris whom Descartes regarded as an enemy, asked one of his correspondents in Leiden to send him sheets as they came off the presses, and managed to obtain a copy of the work before even

---

[30] Baillet, *Vie*, 1. 275.

Descartes's friends; he it was who forwarded it to the mathematician Pierre de Fermat, another of Descartes's adversaries, probably to stimulate a critical reaction to the work. In the end, it seems that only one edition of 500 copies was printed, including the 200 which Descartes received for distribution to his friends; and even these did not sell well. On receiving some corrections to the text from the ever-attentive Mersenne, Descartes wrote on 9 January 1639 that he had gone to this trouble for no purpose: 'in view of the few copies the bookseller says he has sold,' he wrote, 'I see no great likelihood of his having to print it again' (AT 2. 481). The same fate awaited the Elzevier edition of the *Meditations* of 1641. According to one source, Le Maire's edition was not even sold out at the time of Descartes's death; but the Latin version, which appeared with Descartes's blessing in 1644, was eagerly purchased by the scholarly community throughout Europe, and was a commercial success. Le Maire himself was to publish the *Geometry* in Latin in 1649, which may well have given him a better return on his investment than did the *Discourse*. This reveals that the choice of the vernacular restricted the dissemination of the first publication of the *Discourse*; but it may also be that it reflects Descartes's own narrow expectations about its circulation.[31]

The Discourse

As has already been intimated, and will become even clearer below, Descartes did not envisage a single readership for his book; it was explicitly aimed at both his 'scientific' and philosophical colleagues, and a broader constituency of more or less well-educated men and women with an interest in the intellectual life of their day. These would have included members of the professional classes, legal and court officials, surgeons, merchants, and (increasingly) their wives and daughters, together with other literate persons having access to vernacular publications. These readers were served by institutions such as the Bureau d'Adresse, and by popularizing 'scientific' works

[31] Gaukroger, *Descartes*, 321–2, 331–2; F. E. Sutcliffe, *Descartes: Discourse on Method and the Meditations* (Harmondsworth, 1968), 'Introduction', p. 14

such as Mersenne's *New Questions* of 1634 and Charles Sorel's (1599?–1674) *The Knowledge of Material Things* (*La Science des choses corporelles*), which appeared in the same year. The famous opening remark of the *Discourse* about 'good sense' and its equal distribution strongly suggests that what he is going to say will be accessible to all; but the introduction to the essay entitled *Geometry* makes the dual nature of his readership explicit: 'Up to this point I have tried to make myself understood to everyone; but, with regard to this treatise, I am afraid that it cannot be read except by those who already know what is to be found in the books of geometry; for, given that they contain so many well-proven truths, and thinking that it would be superfluous to repeat them, I have not failed to make use of them' (AT 6. 368). It might be concluded from this, and from his claim at the very beginning of the *Discourse* that 'the power of judging correctly and of distinguishing the true from the false is naturally equal in all men', that Descartes imagined that everyone might attain to all knowledge, given the proper training, but that is clearly not the case, as his comment in Part Five reveals: 'as much inequality is found among animals of the same species as among men, and some are easier to train than others' (AT 6. 58); his scathing assessments of his fellow mathematicians seem also to be based on their (alleged) inequality of intellect to his own.

Part Six: The Presentation of the Project

The *Discourse* is somewhat unusual for its day, in that it does not open with a dedicatory letter to a prominent figure, and has no formal preface addressed to the reader to prepare him for what is to come. In so far as such prefatory material is present in the work, it is to be found in the last part of the *Discourse*, called by Descartes its 'description' in the letter of July 1633, quoted above. It is appropriate to consider this first, as it is here that he introduces the work in the traditional way known as the 'access to the author' (*accessus ad auctorem*). This included the moral presentation of a writer (in Descartes's case, it is self-presentation), giving his name (or in Descartes's case, suppressing it), the work's title, the motive for its publication, the ordering of its material, the dignity and utility of its subject-matter, and the genre to which it belongs. Normally this would be done by a lecturer presenting the work of another writer; but there are precedents of self-presentation from the ancient world which were known to his contemporaries: one of these was afforded by the ancient Greek medical writer Galen, whose account of his own work is made up of a very un-Cartesian mixture of argument, polemic, anecdote, autobiography, and digression. Some Renaissance authors also produced works at the end of their lives which offered such an introduction. The famous Dutch humanist Erasmus was one of these; another was Girolamo Cardano (1501–76), who is closer to being a model for Descartes, in that his name was not already widely known when he produced the first version of the *De libris propriis*, a treatise on his own writings, and who, like Descartes, sought to write a radical new account of the whole of philosophy; but there is no indication that Descartes ever read much of his work attentively[32] (although he had almost certainly heard of him, if only through Gabriel Naudé, who in the turbulent Paris of the 1620s was his defender against charges of magic, and eventually the editor of his autobiography). Cardano was more notorious than famous, having been attacked as a libertine writer by the intemperate Jesuit François Garasse (1585–1631) in his anti-libertine *Curious Doctrine of the Wits (or Supposed To Be Such) of Our Time*, published in 1624. Interestingly, Cardano relates a number of his dreams in *On My Own Books*, one of which he looked on as particularly prophetic, as it helped form his sense of destiny as a writer; we may contrast this with Descartes's studious silence on the same matter.[33]

Descartes's intellectual autobiography (Part One of the *Discourse*), which I shall consider below, had already sketched out how he arrived at his general project; Part Six concerns the narrower question of the motivation which first led him to abandon the idea of

---

[32] But see *Geometry*, AT 6. 471–3, where a passage from Cardano's *Ars magna* of 1545 (a mathematical work) is discussed. I am grateful to Noel Malcolm for pointing this out to me.

[33] On *accessus*, see Ian Maclean, *Cardano: De libris propriis* (Milan, 2004), 'Introduction', pp. 13–16, 22–3; on Cardano, see Gabriel Naudé, *Apologie pour tous les grands personnages qui ont esté faussement soupçonnez de magie* (Paris, 1625).

publishing, and then to make him change his mind. Convention-
ally enough, Descartes claims that it is everyone's duty to benefit
their fellow men if they can; he aspires to offer an example of
reaching the truth through the secure grounding of principles, and
the careful checking of further conclusions by engaging in observations and experiments which settle which of various possible
alternative interpretations is to be preferred. His answer to the
question of which branch of learning he is setting out to serve is
ambitious: he suggests that his work will contribute to metaphysics, mathematics, mechanics, and physics. He is looking to secure
practical benefits for his fellow man (not least in the field of
optical-instrument making); and eventually he hopes that all this
will allow him to make progress in medicine, as the restoration and
maintenance of health and the prevention of the effects of ageing
seem to him to have a place among the highest goods of life. He is
severe in his judgement of ill-considered collaboration, which he
believes will lead to time-wasting; and he is horrified at the prospect that his ideas will be taken up by thinkers who do not proceed with his mental rigour and discipline, but will claim to be
working with him. Earlier in the *Discourse* he had poured scorn on
'those who, believing themselves cleverer than they are, cannot
stop themselves jumping to conclusions, and do not have enough
patience to govern their thoughts in an orderly way, with the result
that once they have allowed themselves to doubt accepted principles and stray from the common path, they would never be able
to keep to the road that one must take to proceed in the right
direction, and would remain lost all their lives' (AT 6. 15). This
provides him with another motive for publication: that of wishing
to eliminate, or at least reduce, the risk of misrepresentation, at
the same time as setting out his own achievements. His final
remarks are devoted to justifying his choice of French rather than
Latin: he believes that this will send out a signal that he is interested only in the expression of pure reason, and wishes to show
this by making no allegation of the authority of others, and by
eschewing the use of the language of his teachers and of the international community of natural philosophers. This last decision
certainly brought him a new class of reader in France; but it did

not give him the desired exposure to his 'scientific' colleagues, and led him to revert to writing in Latin, and to agree to the translation of the *Discourse* a few years later. His preoccupation with language (shared with some of his contemporaries, including the author of the prospectus on a new linguistic project he discusses with Mersenne in a letter dated 20 November 1629: AT 1. 76–82) may be linked to his development of a new and more elegant mathematical notation, which is one of the achievements of the essays which accompany the *Discourse*.

Parts One and Two: Intellectual Autobiography

I quoted above from the letter in which Guez de Balzac urged Descartes to set down the 'story of his mind'. Descartes and his contemporaries would have been aware of the existence of such accounts, from Augustine's *Confessions* to Montaigne's chapter on his own education in the *Essays* (1. 26). Descartes's approach to autobiography is innovative in various respects. He does not relate his progress to his temperament, although in letters he talks about his weakly physical disposition as a child and the bellicose humour he attributed to himself in his early manhood (AT 4. 220–1; 2. 480). This is very much an intellectual autobiography; it refers in passing to the staunchness of his religious faith, but mainly concerns his mind. If we recall that in the *Meditations* he defined thinking in a broad way—doubting, understanding, affirming, denying, willing, not willing, imagining, having sensory perceptions (AT 7. 28)—we can understand why he chose to portray his development by including in it a broad account of his mental life. He calls it a story or fable, and later disclaims any intention of inculcating precepts for living; in this he resembles Montaigne, who also insists that he is not teaching, but telling a story, and is doing so principally for himself. But he also suggests, as does Montaigne, that everyone should engage in a similar process, and that others might at least learn from this narrative of his life what ought to be avoided. He admits that he hopes to learn from the public's reaction to his account, just as the ancient Greek painter Apelles had learnt what others made of his paintings by hiding behind them and eavesdropping on their comments (AT 6. 4). He insists further that he is

speaking without the benefit of the divine inspiration which theologians possess: here we may suspect him of coyness about his own
vocation.[34]

His account of traditional philosophy is scathing: it is a training in
how to impress others, and disguise one's own ignorance; what may
most usefully be learned from it is the ability not to be fooled by its
claims. As we would expect from someone who found all previous
philosophy and 'science' to be unsatisfactory, and who gives such a
negative account of his own education, he declares that what he has
learned comes not from the books of the ancients, but from the great
book of the world. This has taught him to see his upbringing and the
values implicit in the judgements he passes on others in relative
terms, but does not cause him to relativize his own religious beliefs.
Such a rejection of one's education might be seen as a necessary
gesture, arising from the very nature of an intellectual autobiography; but the insult to philosophy goes beyond this, and casts
an odd light on the letter he wrote to one of his Jesuit teachers
(possibly Father Étienne Noël) at the Collège de la Flèche on 14 June
1637, to accompany a presentation copy of the *Discourse* (AT 1. 383–
4). In it he thanks the addressee for inculcating in him the first seeds
of philosophy and letters, offers him his book as a tribute to his time
at La Flèche, and invites him to communicate any corrections to its
author, in apparent blithe unawareness that the account he gives of
his philosophical training at that very establishment might be found
offensive.

Parts Two and Three: Precepts in Philosophy and Ethics

The *Discourse* is not about *all* method, but *the* method required for
the 'scientific' investigation of nature. Descartes knew of some
past attempts to find a universal method: he mentions that of the
medieval theologian Raymond Llull (1232–?1315), which he clearly
deems to be a failure, and refers to another attempt—possibly that
of the sixteenth-century French philosopher Pierre de la Ramée
(1515–72)—with a little more respect; but he does not mention other
more recent projects which set out to avoid the allegedly cumbrous

---

[34] Montaigne, *Essais*, 3.2, pp. 804–6: also n. 6, above.

baggage of Aristotelian thought, including that of Francis Bacon. Although he clearly has himself devised a method, he claims not to give an account it; instead, he offers two sets of precepts which he uses as ways of dealing with the error which may exist in his own mind, of building the foundations he needs to make progress in his own work, and of dealing with everyday moral problems as these arise, knowing that for the time being anything certain in such a discipline was unobtainable. The first set concerned the preliminary discipline to which he subjected his mental habits. He resolved 'never to accept anything as true that I did not *incontrovertibly* know to be so; that is to say, carefully to avoid both *prejudice* and premature conclusions; and to include nothing in my judgements other than that which presented itself to my mind so *clearly* and *distinctly*, that I would have no occasion to doubt it'; second, 'to divide all the difficulties under examination into as many parts as possible, and as many as were required to solve them in the best way'; third, 'to conduct my thoughts in a given order, beginning with the *simplest* and most easily understood objects, and gradually ascending, as it were step by step, to the knowledge of the most *complex*; and *positing* an order even on those which do not have a natural order of precedence'; fourth, 'to undertake such complete enumerations and such general surveys that I would be sure to have left nothing out' (AT 6. 18).

His contemporaries would have recognized some of the procedures of traditional philosophy here; division and definition, for example, are processes whereby analysis of an object is undertaken; and exhaustive enumeration of a field of enquiry is itself not a novel precept, being one of the the three laws of predication (*kata pantos*: see Aristotle, *Posterior Analytics*, i.4, 73a 21 ff.); but the categories *incontrovertible, prejudice, clear and distinct*, and *simple and complex* are here subtly different. Incontrovertibility (*évidence, evidentia*) in the traditional sense is a feature of propositions derived from the senses which form the basis of syllogistic demonstration, whereas for Descartes it is to do with the immediacy of mental perception which is not reducible to logical form, and which is 'clear and distinct' of itself; prejudice, for scholastic philosophers, is described in more positive terms as the prior knowledge of facts, or the meanings of words, or both (*praenotio*), and presupposed knowledge in the form of metaphysical principles and categories (form, matter, and privation, act and potency, the four causes, for example), whereas Descartes sees all such mental baggage as noxious; the passage from *simple* to *complex* is seen in traditional terms as one from 'things better known to us [through the senses]' to 'things known by their nature'; this is explicitly reversed by Descartes in the title to the second edition of the *Meditations*, which reads 'On the Nature of the Human Mind, and That It Is Better Known Than the Body'. Here, and elsewhere, Descartes is dissociating his approach to knowledge from the famous Aristotelian adage 'there is nothing in the mind that was not first in the senses' (*nil in intellectu quod non prius fuerit in sensu*). The passage from simple to complex is described usually in terms of the relationship of terms to propositions. Descartes, on the other hand, is concerned with the rigorous development of knowledge from its foundations, or the passage from elements to compounds. Even 'not leaving anything out' separates his undertaking from that of some branches of natural philosophy, in which nature is recognized to have residues and redundancies which would prevent its investigation in any formal mathematical way. Finally, 'positing' is for Descartes not a procedure within logic by which a given proposition is taken for the purposes of argument to be true; his supposition is much closer to a step in the hypothetico–deductive method, the formulation of a hypothesis, consistent with general principles, which then needs to be tested against empirical observations.[35]

The moral code, which has to be put in place because there can be no certainty in this area until the problems of epistemology (the theory of knowledge) and ontology (the theory of being) have been sorted out, is in a similar way a combination of the familiar and the new. The first rule is 'to obey the laws and customs of my country, and to adhere to the religion in which God by his grace had me instructed from my childhood, and to govern myself in everything

---

[35] On these terms, see Étienne Gilson, *Index scolastico-cartésien* (Paris, 1979); Jean-Luc Marion, *Descartes: 'Règles utiles et claires pour la direction de l'esprit en la recherche de la vérité'* (The Hague, 1977), glossary.

else according to the most moderate and least extreme opinions, being those commonly received among the wisest of those with whom I should have to live'; this makes reference to the virtue of prudence, which in classical ethics governs moral and political behaviour. The acceptance of custom, which Montaigne also advocated, gives value to entrenched social practices, and creates a predisposition to see moral and political values in local and relative terms, which Descartes makes explicit in the text of the *Discourse*. The second and third rules are recognizably neo-Stoic:

to be as firm and resolute in my actions as I could, and to follow no less constantly the most doubtful opinions, once I had opted for them, than I would have if they had been the most certain ones; to endeavour always to master myself rather than fortune, to try to change my desires rather than to change the order of the world, and in general to settle for the belief that there is nothing entirely in our power except our thoughts, and after we have tried, in respect of things external to us, to do our best, everything in which we do not succeed is absolutely impossible as far as we are concerned.

These rules recall strongly the opening sentences of the *Enchiridion* (a handbook of moral philosophy) of the ancient Stoic philosopher-slave Epictetus:

Some things are in our control and others not. Things in our control are opinion, pursuit, desire, aversion, and, in a word, whatever are our own actions. Things not in our control are body, property, reputation, command, and, in one word, whatever are not our own actions. The things in our control are by nature free, unrestrained, unhindered; but those not in our control are weak, slavish, restrained, belonging to others. Remember, then, that if you suppose that things which are slavish by nature are also free, and that what belongs to others is your own, then you will be hindered. You will lament, you will be disturbed, and you will find fault both with gods and men. But if you suppose that only to be your own which is your own, and what belongs to others such as it really is, then no one will ever compel you or restrain you. Further, you will find fault with no one or accuse no one. You will do nothing against your will. No one will hurt you, you will have no enemies, and you not be harmed.

Such a philosophy of self-sufficiency was popularized in France in the years following its calamitous religious wars by such writers as Guillaume Du Vair (1556–1621), who translated Epictetus into French, and whose frequently reprinted book *On Constancy* (1594) aspires to reconcile ancient Stoicism with Christianity, and stresses the importance of controlling the will and developing a personal philosophy as an antidote to the vicissitudes of fortune, the evils of the times, and the uncertainty of happiness. An international scholar who had himself published a work with the title *De constantia* in 1584, and who had much to do with the dissemination of these ideas, was Justus Lipsius; his *Introduction to Stoic Philosophy* (*Manuductio ad stoicam philosophiam*) appeared in 1604. The similarity of these programmes to that put forward to Descartes is very striking; he was to take its self-determining implications even further in his *Passions of the Soul*, where he claims that 'there is no soul so feeble that, correctly governed, cannot acquire an absolute mastery over its passions' (AT 11. 368–70).

Part Four: Metaphysics and Epistemology

Descartes was very aware that his metaphysics and epistemology, as well as the account of nature which flowed from them, were very radical. He did not think that this would be as much a problem for those amongst his readers who were not university-educated, and who would have no vested interest in protecting entrenched philosophical positions; but even in their case, when he came to introduce the first part of the *Meditations*, he advised them to 'devote several months, or at least weeks, to considering the topics dealt with, before going on' (AT 7. 130). He rightly saw that the learned community, who would be more familiar with the material, would find what he had to say even more difficult to accept. Writing to Mersenne on 28 January 1641, he expressed the hope 'that my readers will get used to my principles without perceiving that they are doing so, and before they notice that my principles destroy those of Aristotle' (AT 3. 298). Whereas the implicit message—that anyone could undertake the journey of self-discovery and the discovery of God and the world—would be seen as liberating by non-specialist readers, professional philosophers would balk at a form of reasoning that could not be reduced to syllogistic logic, would reject a representation of the thinking human being which ignored almost all of traditional faculty psychology, and would jib at baffling new accounts of the soul, of the relationship of mind to body, and of that of matter to thought and action.

There is a massive philosophical literature on the aspect of Descartes's thought which is summarily expounded in Part Four of the *Discourse*, and set out with great care in the *Meditations*; I shall indicate in the Explanatory Notes specific difficulties that were perceived by his learned contemporaries in what he has to say. I want here to indicate what was seen to be problematic in general terms. Part Four opens by applying 'methodical doubt' to human claims for knowledge of any kind; this has been linked to the vogue for scepticism in Descartes's day, and has been seen as his answer to a crisis in early modern thought, in which Descartes used the favoured weapon of atheists against themselves. This account is now seen as not wholly satisfactory. There is, after all, nothing particularly new in beginning a quest for certainty by calling into question as much as one can, and certainty is indisputably Descartes's quarry: 'there are already so many views in philosophy which are no more than plausible and which can be maintained in debate,' he wrote in the letter to Mersenne in November 1633 cited above, 'that if my views have no greater certainty than that and cannot be approved of without controversy, I refuse ever to publish them' (AT 1. 271–2; also 1. 331–2). 'Approved of without controversy' refers to what in Descartes's day was known as 'probable' knowledge; this epithet was mainly used at this time to indicate not a judgement of relative frequency, but an argument from authority based on the judgement of the experts in any given field. Descartes clearly had no time for other experts, but still evokes here the principle of uncontroversially approved knowledge, as he believes that his own metaphysical foundations will command assent once they are known.

In traditional terms, certainty was established by the use of syllogistic logic; in its place, Descartes uses a form of immediate intuition which cannot be reduced to proposition, middle term, and conclusion. One of the standard scholastic examples of the strongest (first) figure of syllogistic reasoning is the following:

| Everything having large extremities is strong | (all B is A) |
| All lions have large extremities | (all C is B) |

| All lions are strong | (all C is A) |

When Descartes was invited later in his life to consider setting out his philosophy in such conventional terms, he first argued that it would be an immensely inefficient way of doing so ('if I had decided to deduce all of this in the form of logical argument, I would have worn out the hands of the printers and the eyes of my readers by producing a huge tome', he wrote to one of his correspondents in October 1637: AT 1. 423–4); later, in an interview he gave to the young Dutch scholar Frans Burman (1628–79), he went further, and contended that it was not only a cumbersome, but also an erroneous, way to do it (AT 5. 147). Burman wondered whether the 'cogito' (Descartes's assertion that 'I am thinking therefore I exist'—(cogito ergo sum) was reducible to a syllogism in the following form:

Whatever is thinking exists
I am thinking

Therefore I exist

Descartes had already refuted this reductive account in his reply to the second set of Objections to the *Meditations*:

When someone says 'I am thinking therefore I am or exist', he does not deduce existence from thought by means of a syllogism but recognizes it as something self-evident by a simple intuition of the mind, as is clear from the fact that if he were deducing existence by means of a syllogism, he would have to have had previous knowledge of the major premise 'Everything which is thinking is, or exists'; yet in fact he rather learns it from experiencing in himself that it is impossible for him to think without existing. (AT 7. 140)

His opponents retorted that when his arguments were translated into traditional syllogistic terms, they were exposed as circular.[36]

Even if some of his contemporaries were prepared to accept the immediacy of the intuition 'I am thinking, therefore I am', they still found problems with the version of mind and of self-enquiry which it implies. In traditional terms, the intellect as it thinks is present in the human being in at least two modes, active and passive; it is part of a complex procedure of retrieving and transmitting knowledge, which begins with the image (*species*) of the object intended by the intellect, which passes into the brain through the senses, is gathered in a 'common sense' (*sensus communis*) that pools all the information available, then translated into intelligible form by the passive intellect, and finally taken up as a concept by the agent intellect. This version of perception is hylomorphic: that is, it combines matter and form, the sensible and the intelligible. Descartes, on the other hand, insists on the immaterial character of all thought. The mental faculties of reason, imagination, and memory are located in traditional terms in the ventricles of the brain, both imagination and memory having a material component; Descartes refers to these faculties, but categorizes them as 'thinking substance' (*res cogitans*), and denies them material being or locality. The immaterial thinking ego is set against the material world, which is no longer described in terms of elements in various combinations and compositions, but instead only as 'extended substance' (*res extensa*). The second half of the formula 'I am thinking, therefore I am' is an affirmation by Descartes not only of essence, but also of existence; in traditional terms, essence and existence are separately conceived. What Descartes says was not unintelligible to his contemporaries, but it was profoundly radical; it dispensed with many of the presuppositions of Aristotelian metaphysics and psychology.[37]

[36] See John Cottingham, *Descartes* (Oxford and Carlton, Va., 1986), 36–7 (on the *cogito* in syllogistic form), 66–70 (on the circle); Louis E. Loeb, 'The Cartesian Circle', in *The Cambridge Companion to Descartes*, ed. John Cottingham (Cambridge, 1992), 200–35; and Étienne Gilson, *René Descartes: Discours de la méthode: texte et commentaire*, Paris, 1962)) 360–2.

[37] See the various contributions in *The Cambridge History of Renaissance Philosophy* ed. Charles B. Schmitt, Quentin Skinner, and Eckhard Kessler (Cambridge, 1988) 453–638.

Some of Descartes's first readers were not convinced of the novelty of his proof of God's existence, which follows from the intuition of his own. These critics pointed to the similarity of the 'cogito' to an argument in St Augustine, and indicated the (probably unfair) parallel which might be drawn between the famous ontological proof of God's existence (the argument that the concept of God entails His real existence, first formulated by St Anselm and best known through its rehearsal in Aquinas's *Summa Theologiae*) and Descartes's argument that the ego's intuition of its imperfection necessarily implies knowledge of a pre-existent perfect deity. His claim that the soul is immaterial was also seen as not particularly novel; it touched upon a very active contemporary debate concerning the immortality of the soul. Various exegetes of Aristotle, most notably the medieval Arabic philosopher Averroes and the second-century commentator Alexander of Aphrodisias (whose relevant works had first been made available in the fifteenth century), had argued that Aristotle held the soul to be material, and to die with the body; this view was declared to be heretical by the Church at various times, notably in a decree of the Fifth Lateran Council of 1513, which required all Christian philosophers to demonstrate through philosophical (not theological) argument that the soul was immortal and immaterial. The offending interpreter of Aristotle at that time was the Italian professor Pietro Pomponazzi (1462–1524); his treatise on the subject was reissued in 1634, probably in Paris, in the wake of the libertine ferment of the 1620s. This had provoked a reaction in the form of a number of vernacular defences of the soul's immortality and Aristotle's subscription to this belief, including those by the Jesuit Louis Richeome (1544–1625) and Descartes's acquaintance Jean de Silhon. Descartes himself was made aware by Mersenne of some of the materialist libertine tracts circulating more or less clandestinely in Paris (AT 1. 144, 148, 181, 220), and, in the introduction to his *Meditations* of 1641, was to make reference to the decree of 1513 and to the need to argue for the soul's immortality (AT 7. 3); in fact he does not set out here to prove more than its *immateriality*. But it may have been the currency of the debate about the soul's *immortality* which caused Mersenne to add the words to the title of the first, Parisian, edition of the *Meditations*, 'in which the existence of God and the immortality of the soul are demonstrated' (AT 3. 239); these were changed in the subsequent Amsterdam edition of 1642, for which Descartes was responsible, to the more accurate claim: 'in which the existence of God and the distinction between the human soul and the body are demonstrated.' The earlier version of the title shows how Descartes's work could be reduced against the wishes of its author to the terms of a current debate, and its novelty and precision misrepresented.[38]

Part Five: Physics and Physiology

Descartes's two planned works, *The Universe* and *Man*, were to have been an account of a new departure in natural philosophy. There had been radical rethinkings before him of Aristotelian physics: in a letter to Beeckman of 17 October 1630, Descartes himself mentions such names as Bernardino Telesio (1509–88), Giordano Bruno, and Tommaso Campanella (AT 1. 158), although that does not indicate necessarily that he had read their works attentively (or at all). In Part Five of the *Discourse*, Descartes sets out in very summary terms the argument of his *Universe*, gives an account of the operation of the heart, and sets down his theory of the difference between animals and man. Various elements of mechanical philosophy emerge from these accounts: first, all natural phenomena proceed from a combination of matter and movement, and can be explained in terms of shape, size, quantity, and motion; second, all natural beings operate like machines, and obey universal physical laws which are reducible to mathematical terms; third, all bodies are made up of corpuscles which are too small to be perceived, which (depending on the theor-

---

[38] Both Mersenne (as revealed by Descartes's letter to him of 25 May 1637: AT 1. 376), and Antoine Arnauld in his objections to the *Meditations* (AT 7. 197) point to the fact that a similar argument appears at various points in St Augustine's writings: *De libero arbitrio*, 2. 3. 7; *De civitate Dei*, 9. 26; also *De trinitate*, 10. 10. 14. On the immortality of the soul, see Eckhard Kessler, 'The intellective soul', in *The Cambridge History of Renaissance Philosophy*, 485–534. Descartes's determination that the memory is immaterial removes one of the difficulties of conceiving of the individual soul after death, as in traditional terms its separation from the body would have removed access to the memory which was materially located in it: see the letter to Huygens of 10 Oct. 1642 (AT 3. 598).

ist) may or may not be infinitely divisible, and may circulate either in a plenum or in a vacuum (the former of these alternatives being Descartes's claim).

In his later works, Descartes was to elaborate a mechanical philosophy which was axiomatic in structure, running from the simplest principles of human knowledge in a continuous series; by defining matter solely in terms of extension, he would be able to claim that physics could be based on the geometrical analysis of bodies in motion. Such ideas are not spelt out systematically in the *Discourse*; rather, the operation of the heart and the nature of animals as opposed to man are used to exemplify rather than demonstrate the explanatory force of the mechanical philosophy. Descartes's contemporaries would not have had difficulty in grasping what he says, new though it was, as the letter setting out objections to his ideas possibly written in February 1638 shows (AT 1. 511–17). The areas he discusses were widely debated at the time (he himself refers to Harvey's book on the circulation of the blood, to which he grants qualified approval, unlike many of his contemporaries); the issues involved were well known to both Aristotelians and those who were interested in ancient atomism, such as Pierre Gassendi (1592–1655), the author of the fifth set of Objections to the *Meditations* (AT 7. 257–346). In Descartes's account, the role of the animal spirits as particles which pass through a specific gland (the pineal gland) in the brain, where the immaterial soul can interact with them, is crucial to his mechanical model of the human body. Descartes sets out here in a worked example what he was able later, in his *Principles of Philosophy* of 1644, to offer in general terms, in a form somewhere between a textbook and a sequence of demonstrations in the manner of classical geometry, as a radical and coherent alternative to the natural philosophy he had been taught at school.[39]

---

[39] William Harvey, *Exercitatio anatomica de motu cordis et sanguinis in animalibus* (Frankfurt, 1628) English translation, *An Anatomical Disputation Concerning the Movement of the Heart and Blood in Living Creatures*, trans. and introd. Gweneth Whitteridge (Oxford, 1976); Daniel Garber, *Descartes's Metaphysical Physics* (Chicago, 1992).

The Essays Published With the Discourse: Dioptrics,
Meteorology, Geometry

It is important to remember that the book that came on to the market
in 1637 was not a slim pamphlet delineating the whole of Descartes's
philosophy: it was a stout quarto of more than 500 pages, including
three essays illustrated with expensive diagrams, to which the opening discourse was a brief introduction, intended to illustrate the
benefits of Descartes's new way of thinking and rigorous method.
The first two of these essays are addressed to the general reader (who
would have been able to follow the *Discourse*, as I have tried to show);
the *Dioptrics* addresses in turn the physical nature of light, refraction
(the law of which, as has already been pointed out, Descartes was not
alone in discovering in his generation), the physiology and optics of
the eye, the relation of the senses to the nervous system and the
brain, retinal images, vision, and the means of its correction. In
accordance with his programmatic claim that man could enhance his
understanding and exploitation of nature by invention, Descartes
considers finally the best technique for grinding lenses, and their
optimum shape.

   The *Meteorology* addresses various phenomena—clouds, mists,
and miasma; rain, hail, and snow; storms, thunder, and lightning;
celestial events such as the appearance of 'false' suns (parhelia)—
with a view to discovering explanations of them which do not rely
on supernatural intervention of any kind, and accord with Descartes's physics, which is anti-atomistic. There are also discourses
on salts, rainbows, and colours. The subject-matter and the questions considered have much in common with Aristotle's *Meteorology*
and the relevant section of his *Problems*; Descartes even refers at one
point, in an apparently conciliatory way, to scholastic discussions
derived from these texts: 'In order to remain at peace with [trad-
itional] philosophers, I don't at all want to go against what they
imagine to be in these bodies in addition to what I have spoken of,
such as their *substantial forms* and *real qualities* and suchlike, but it
seems to me that my arguments should be more acceptable in that I
have made them depend on fewer things' (AT 6. 239). It is not
difficult to detect the scorn behind this remark directed at such

metaphysical baggage; this is made explicit in a letter to Regius of January 1642, in which Descartes takes his disciple to task for rejecting substantial forms and real qualities in a polemical way, and recommends that he follow the less confrontational strategy of the *Meteorology* by producing new arguments without rejecting or denying traditional accounts, simply setting these aside as unnecessary for current explanatory purposes (AT 3. 492). The nature of the phenomena discussed by Descartes was also debated in French in the Bureau d'Adresse, and by Mersenne in his *Questions*; but Descartes's minimalist processes of explanation contrast with what is to be found either there, or in such successful works as Cornelis Drebbel's (1572–1634) *Treatise on the Nature of the Elements*, which first appeared some twenty years before, and was widely diffused in various languages.[40]

In the final section of the *Discourse*, Descartes comments on the proof system of the first two essays in the following way: 'it seems to me that my arguments follow each other in such a way that if the last are proven by the first, which are their causes, the first are reciprocally proved by the last, which are their effects' (AT 6. 76). This would have struck a chord with contemporary natural philosophers, who were aware of a logical procedure known as *regressus*, by which a proof whose conclusion is a cause (*demonstratio quia*) is translated into one whose conclusion is an effect (*demonstratio propter quid*), the latter being superior, as it is more 'scientific' to argue from causes than from effects. Its standard example in natural philosophy is the following:

Demonstratio quia	Major	Non-twinkling things are near
	Minor (effect)	Planets are non-twinkling things
	Conclusion (cause)	Planets are near

---

[40] See above, n. 24; Drebbel appeared in Dutch, German, and Latin between 1608 and 1628 at various printing centres.

Demonstratio propter quid	Major	What is near is non-twinkling
	Minor (cause)	Planets are near
	Conclusion (effect)	Planets do not twinkle

The passage from the first to the second syllogism marks also the passage from the 'order of discovery' (*ordo inveniendi*) to the 'order of teaching' (*ordo docendi*). It has already been pointed out that the *Meditations* ask the reader to follow the process of discovery; not, however, from objective effects but from subjective intuition. When Descartes sets out proofs in the three essays which follow the *Discourse*, he explicitly uses the model of geometrical presentation (from axioms upwards), which is pedagogical, but not in the manner of natural philosophy. It may seem that the rationalist Descartes is engaged in something similar to *regressus*, but in fact he is not: he wants his premises to be causal, and he argues from effect only to confirm the cause, by a process akin to the hypothetico–deductive method mentioned above, as he makes clear in a letter to Morin dated 13 July 1638 (AT 2. 197–8). This contrasts sharply with the practice of the English empirical natural philosophers who were his near-contemporaries, such as William Harvey, Thomas Willis, Robert Hooke, and Robert Boyle. Much later, the novelist André Gide produced in the mouth of one of his characters an ironic comment on this process: 'I'm willing for reality to support my thinking, like a proof, but not for it to precede it.'[41]

The third of the trio of essays, *Geometry*, is perhaps the most far-reaching. Descartes is here no longer addressing the non-specialist, as his note to the reader (quoted above) shows. He does not always make life easy even for his mathematically adept readers, for he also wilfully omits some of the steps of his demonstrations and some of their consequences, as his final comment reveals: 'I hope that future

[41] Aristotle, *Posterior Analytics*, i. 13 78a 22–17a16; Nicholas Jardine, 'The Epistemology of the Sciences', in *The Cambridge History of Renaissance Philosophy*, 686–93; Gide, *Les Faux-monnayeurs*, ed. J. C. Davies (London, 1986), 428: 'je consens que la réalité vienne à l'appui de la pensée, comme une preuve, mais non point qu'elle la précède.'

generations will be grateful to me not only for the things I have explained in these pages, but also for those I have deliberately left out, in order to leave them the pleasure of discovering them' (AT 6. 485). Whether some of his correspondents were grateful to him for setting problems either too difficult for them, or lacking all the information necessary for a solution, is another question. This short work marks the moment—presaged in works by various other mathematicians, or actually accomplished before this date in unpublished writings such as those of Thomas Harriot (1560?–1621)—at which geometry and algebra ceased being separate. Descartes's treatise makes connections between algebra and geometry which enable the solution of algebraic problems geometrically, and geometrical problems algebraically; it is the precursor of what now would be called 'analytical geometry'. Descartes's mathematics is presented in a more elegant, flexible, and developable notation than used by previous generations, with a more successful use of diagrams, and a broader range of expressions, including those for negative and imaginary numbers and variables. Whereas most of the rest of his work, whether physical or philosophical, has been challenged or discredited, parts of the mathematics have proved to be an enduring intellectual legacy.[42]

Descartes as a Writer

It would not be appropriate here to engage in a detailed analysis of Descartes's French, but it is pertinent to point to one or two features of his style. It has often been praised for its clarity and restraint; indeed, it contrasts markedly with that of his friend Guez de Balzac, which is orotund and florid by comparison. Another writer of similarly lucid and rigorous French, a century before, was the reformer Jean Calvin (1509–64): like Descartes, he had undergone a training in the law, which had bred in him caution and subtlety in his use of causal connectives, negatives, disjunctives, and conjunctives, and had made him aware of the distinction between proper and

---

[42] On Harriot, see *Thomas Harriot: An Elizabethan Man of Science*, ed. Robert Fox (Aldershot, 2000).

improper signification, the pitfalls of definition, and the vices of ambiguity and obscurity. This caution is detectable in Descartes's clear but complex syntax; he has a predilection for subordinate clauses and qualifications; he shows great care in expressing preconditions and causal relations, often preferring the weakest designations—'for', 'in so far as', 'seeing that'—to 'since' and 'because'; and he is very adept in the use of negation, double negation, and even on occasion triple negation. These features of his style, which to a small degree have been attenuated in this translation in the interests of ease of reading, also reflect his precise and fastidious nature, with its preoccupation with truth and accuracy.

There are clear signs that he was trying to write accessibly and attractively; this is most evident in his use of sustained images. As one would expect, Descartes has recourse to the commonplace metaphor of philosophy as a building, although in a more restrained way than that of some of his contemporaries, as illustrated by a comparison with this passage from Galileo's *Dialogue*. In it, the Italian physicist has the enlightened modern philosopher Sagredo express his ironic sympathy for the hidebound scholastic Simplicio:

I pity Simplicio no less than I should some gentleman, who, having built a magnificent palace at great trouble and expense, employing myriads of artisans, and then seeing it threatened with ruin because of poor foundations, should attempt, in order to avoid the sad sight of walls destroyed, adorned as they are with so many lovely murals; or columns fall, which support the superb galleries, or gilded beams collapse, or doors, pediments and marble cornices, supplied at so much cost, spoiled—should attempt to prevent the collapse with chains, props, buttresses, iron bars, and shores.[43]

In a similar way, Descartes quite frequently refers to the dangers of building on poor foundations (indeed, the *Meditations* open with a

---

[43] Galileo, *Dialogo sopra i due massimi sistemi del mondo*, in *Opere*, ed. Ferdinando Flora (Milan, and Naples, 1953), I. 412–3: 'io compatisco, [il signor Simplicio], non meno che a quel signore che, con gran tempo, con spesa immensa, con l'opera di cento e cento artefici, fabbricò nobilissimo palazzo, e poi lo vegga, per esser stato mal fondato, minacciar rovina, e che, per non vedere con tanto cordoglio disfatte le mura di tante vaghe pitture adornate, cadute le colonne sostegni delle superbe loggie, caduti i palchi dorati, rovinati gli stipiti, i frontespizi e le cornici marmoree con tanta spesa condotte, cerchi con catene, puntelli, contrafforti, barbacani e sorgozzoni di riparare alla rovina.'

reference to this image: AT 7. 17–18); but he also puts architectural imagery to more personal uses. The laborious and ineffective process of shoring up a philosophical system by its adherents is contrasted in the *Discourse* with the much more successful procedure of planning something anew from the very beginning: 'buildings which a single architect has planned and completed', Descartes avers, 'are usually more beautiful and better designed than those that several architects have tried to patch together, using old walls that had been constructed for other purposes' (AT 6. 11). Galileo does not concern himself with the question whether radical philosophical enterprises are better engaged in collectively or singly; Descartes has no doubt that the latter strategy is preferable, and makes this clear by his reference to the time-wasting involved in working with enthusiastic collaborators, who might either be dim and require much to be explained to them, or alternatively precipitate in their judgements, and bring Cartesianism into disrepute through their ill-considered support of the cause. The sustained analogy between philosophy and architecture is here made economically to serve Descartes's own purposes.

Descartes also states that there is a role for the discarded materials of discredited philosophical systems: just as one usually preserves bits of debris from the old building in order to reuse them in constructing a new one, so also should one, in destroying all those opinions which are judged to be ill-founded, be prepared to reuse some of the elements on which they were based in establishing more certain ones (AT 6. 29). It would seem that this suggestion is not wholly sincere, or rather, it is only sincerely meant in the sphere of ethics and political behaviour. Descartes's advice to Regius not to exacerbate Aristotelians by confrontation where this is not necessary, cited above, must be seen in the light of his private hope that they will not notice the degree to which his thought is inconsistent with that of the prevailing scholasticism. In writing to his Jesuit master at La Flèche, and in seeking the approbation of the Sorbonne (the theological faculty of the University of Paris, to whom he dedicated the *Meditations*) and of that of Father Gibieuf, he seems to be hoping that his own system will replace that of Aristotle, not that it should reconfigure parts of it. The only part of traditional thinking which is clearly retained is its overall arboreal structure (metaphysics as the root, physics as the trunk, and ethics and medicine as the highest branches); but even here, Descartes produces an innovation by having metaphysics considered before physics, whereas in the scholastic curriculum metaphysics was taught later, even if it was looked upon as 'first philosophy'.[44]

One specific feature of the reuse of old philosophical materials which Descartes addresses is lexical. In his metaphysics he employs terms such as 'substance', 'essence', and 'existence', but by making existence a feature of the thinking subject, from whose reflection the existence of God is deduced, he alters radically the traditional relationship between these terms. Equally, his radical separation of the 'thinking substance' and the 'extended substance'—what has come to be known as his dualism—disrupts the semantic coherence of much of the hylomorphic vocabulary of the schoolmen ('form', 'matter', 'substantial form', 'accident', 'quality'). Even the phrase 'clear and distinct' in his usage, denoting what is sufficiently perceptible to the attentive mind to rule out confusion as to what is perceived, is very different from its employment by near-contemporary logicians such as Jacopo Zabarella (1533–89), for whom it describes the effect of the agent intellect on the confused sense impressions that are in the part of the mind designed to receive them (the 'common sense'). The Cartesian modifications of these terms will be discussed in the Notes; the most important of them are italicized in this translation (a practice espoused by Descartes himself, albeit sparingly); there are also other terms that deserve separate mention here, as they would have struck contemporaries as particularly transgressive. The word 'soul' (as opposed to 'mind' or 'rational intellect') does not refer in Descartes to the vitalistic principle or source of life of the scholastics; it is purely mechanical. 'Evidence' is linked by Descartes to his notion of intuition, which he defines in the *Rules* as 'the conception of a clear and attentive mind, which is so easy and distinct that there can be no room for doubt about what we are understanding' (AT 10. 368); for his

---

[44] AT 1. 383–4; letter to Father Guillaume Gibieuf of 11 Nov. 1640 (AT 3. 237–8), cf. AT 3. 184, 328; *Principes*, AT 9B. 14 (on the tree of knowledge).

Aristotelian contemporaries, it is bound into a system of assessing the demonstrative status of propositions, and is often linked to sensory information. Descartes uses terms such as 'plausible' and 'probable' to denote unacceptable levels of uncertainty; his scholastic contemporaries recognized that the degree of truth attainable in various areas of knowledge could never aspire to a higher status than this, and were content with it. Finally, thought, as has been pointed out, is both enriched as a term, designating both the process of knowing and its product, and covering as it does imagining, willing, and so on; and impoverished, as it is cut free from the process by which knowledge is acquired from the senses. The overall effect would have struck Descartes's contemporaries as a form of re-description which is at the same time a re-evaluation, or, to use a term of art from rhetoric which has recently been given some prominence, 'paradiastole'.[45]

As well as the metaphor of architecture, Descartes exploits that of the journey and its parallel with encounters with the past ('conversing with those of another age is more or less the same thing as travelling') and with intellectual progress. From the opening of Seneca's *De vita beata* ('On the Happy Life': a book he recommended to the Princess Elizabeth) he borrows the image of 'those who go forward but very slowly, and who can get further, if they always follow the right road, than those who are in too much of a hurry and stray off it' (AT 6. 2). Elsewhere, he compares himself to 'a man walking by himself in the dark', who decided 'to go so slowly and to exercise such caution in everything that even if he made very little progress, he would at least be sure not to fall' (AT 6. 16–17). To justify his strict adherence to moral decisions once he had reached them, Descartes declares that he:

imitated those travellers who, finding themselves lost in a forest, must not wander in circles first to one side then to the other, and still less stop in one place, but have to walk as straight as possible in one direction, and not alter course for weak reasons, even if it might only have been chance which had led them to settle on the direction they had chosen; for by this

---

[45] See above n. 35; on paradiastole, see Quentin Skinner, 'Thomas Hobbes: Rhetoric and the Construction of Morality', *Proceedings of the British Academy*, 76 (1991), 1–61.

means, even if they do not end up precisely where they want to be, they will eventually reach somewhere where they will most likely be better off than the middle of a forest. (AT 6. 24–5)

There is nothing particularly original about these passages, but they sit comfortably in the *Discourse*, and reinforce its nature as a document accessible to all.

Other images popular in his day find their way into the *Discourse*, and have the same function: the world is a stage on which dramas are played out; philosophers are like 'military commanders whose forces usually grow in proportion to their victories, and who need more skill to maintain their position after defeat in battle than they need to take towns and provinces after a victory. For to try to overcome all the problems and errors that prevent us attaining knowledge of the truth is indeed to engage in battle' (AT 6. 28, 67). Ignorance is darkness or blindness; light is knowledge or insight: 'so it was that I freed myself gradually from many of the errors that can obscure the natural light of our minds'; 'God has given each of us an inner light to distinguish the true from the false'; Aristotelians are 'like blind men who, in order to fight on equal terms against those who can see, lure them into the depths of some very dark cellar'. This last image, like many in Descartes's writing, is a sustained simile: 'I may say that it is in the interest of these people that I abstain from publishing the principles of philosophy that I use; for as they are very simple and very certain, I would be doing the same in publishing them as opening some windows, and letting the light of day into the cellar into which they have gone down to fight' (AT 6. 10, 27, 72). But it is sustained in a very controlled way; unlike Galileo, whose fine building on insecure foundations is expanded for the sake of creating a rich and detailed picture for the pleasure of the reader as opposed to subserving an analogy, Descartes does not allow similes and metaphors to run away with him. They are controlled, sober, and precisely employed, and reflect the thought which they are there to mediate.

Envoi: The Cartesian Philosophical Edifice

Some time ago, a cartoon purporting to illustrate the difference between the French philosophical tradition and Anglo-American analytical philosophy appeared in the pages of the magazine *Punch*. It portrayed French philosophy as a phantasmagorical multi-turreted castle resting precariously on such narrow foundations that the whole image resembled an inverted pyramid; Anglo-American analytical philosophy, by contrast, was represented as a plain brick, on which a philosopher was hesitantly planning to place another. This neatly caricatured the propensity to unfettered rationalist abstract speculation of the French tradition on the one hand, and the over-cautious approach of the Anglo-American tradition on the other—a comparison which the historian of physics Pierre Duhem expressed in terms more favourable to the French, by contrasting their 'profound mind', marked by its penchant for generality and abstraction, with the capacity of the English to see 'picturesque details' in a concrete way, but to compose explanations of given phenomena which may not have any overall coherence.[46]

While it is likely that the British cartoonist had the flights of existentialist fancy of Sartre more in his mind than the work of Descartes, it plausible that he would have seen the latter, a self-declared ambitious system-builder, as a legitimate target also. Yet many distinguished adherents of Anglo-American analytical philosophy recognize Descartes as a founding father of good philosophical practice—the cautious placing of one brick on another, the patient and thorough examination of the validity of arguments—and he is still used as a text on which first-year undergraduates in Great Britain and America are made to cut their teeth. Modern commentators from both sides of the Channel are united in applauding the rigour and discipline of his thought, even if they perceive parts of it to contain errors of reasoning or problems of implication. Descartes's philosophical enterprise is captured by neither component of the cartoonist's caricature, or perhaps by both. He certainly set out to build a whole system which would eventually reach new heights of philosophical achievement, but he also believed in the

[46] Pierre Duhem, *La Théorie physique* (Paris, 1914), 77–154.

need for irrefragable foundations. If he had completed his life's work, he would have hoped to be able to show that from the immediate intuition of the thinking self, a system could be constructed which would offer a way (when combined with the hypothetico-deductive method) both to set about accounting for the natural world as it is, and to manipulate it for man's own ends; at its topmost level it would support a perfect medical science, with its guarantee of health and longevity, and an ultimate version of ethics, with its promise of tranquillity of mind and happiness. This is the programme which the *Discourse* sets out, and which Descartes's subsequent publications confirm. While one must acknowledge that he failed to achieve his philosophical goals, and was wrong in many of his 'scientific' claims, one cannot but admire the intellectual scope and ambition of his enterprise.

NOTE ON THE TEXT

The text which has been used for this translation is that in Descartes, *Œuvres complètes*, ed. Charles Adam and Paul Tannery, 11 vols. (Paris, 1996), referred to as AT in the Introduction and Notes. The *Discours de la méthode* appears in vol. 6, pp. 1–78. It is reproduced by Étienne Gilson, *René Descartes: Discours de la méthode: texte et commentaire* (Paris, 1962).

The marginal numbers refer to the pages of the AT edition. Asterisks signify an editorial note at the back of the book.

SELECT BIBLIOGRAPHY

There is a vast amount of material on Descartes; below are some (mainly English-language) texts which may be found useful among many others.

Editions

Œuvres, 11 vols., ed. Charles Adam and Paul Tannery (Paris, 1996).

The Philosophical Writings Of Descartes, vols. 1 and 2, trans. John Cottingham, Robert Stoothoff, and Dugald Murdoch (Cambridge, 1985); vol. 3, trans. the above and Anthony Kenny (Cambridge, 1991).

Biographies

Adrien Baillet, *La Vie de Monsieur Descartes*, 2 vols. (Paris, 1691).

Stephen Gaukroger, *Descartes: An Intellectual Biography* (Oxford, 1995).

Geneviève Rodis-Lewis, *Descartes: His Life and Thought*, trans. Jane Marie Todd (Ithaca and London, 1998).

General Background

The Cambridge History of Renaissance Philosophy, ed. Charles B. Schmitt, Quentin Skinner, and Eckhard Kessler (Cambridge, 1988).

The Cambridge History of Seventeenth-Century Philosophy, 2 vols., ed. Daniel Garber and Michael Ayers (Cambridge, 1998).

Critical Guides and Secondary Literature

Collections of Essays

The Cambridge Companion to Descartes, ed. John Cottingham (Cambridge, 1992).

Descartes, ed. John Cottingham (Oxford, 1998).

Descartes: A Collection of Critical Essays, ed. Willis Doney (London, 1968).

Descartes: Critical and Interpretive Essays, ed. Michael Hooker (Baltimore and London, 1978).

Reason, Will and Sensation: Essays on Descartes's Metaphysics, ed. John Cottingham (Oxford, 1994).

Stephen Voss, *Essays on the Philosophy and Science of Descartes* (Oxford, 1993).

Individual Studies

Roger Ariew, *Descartes and the Last Scholastics* (Ithaca and London, 1999).

Desmond M. Clarke, *Descartes's Theory of Mind* (Oxford, 2003).

John Cottingham, *Descartes* (Oxford, 1986).

Edwin M. Curley, *Descartes Against the Skeptics* (Oxford, 1978).

Daniel Garber, *Descartes' Metaphysical Physics* (Chicago, 1992).

Stephen Gaukroger, *Descartes' System of Natural Philosophy* (Cambridge, 2002).

Anthony Kenny, *Descartes: A Study of His Philosophy* (Bristol, 1968).

Tom Sorell, *Descartes* (Oxford, 1987).

Bernard Williams, *Descartes: The Project of Pure Enquiry* (Harmondsworth, 1978).

Glossaries

Étienne Gilson, *Index scolastico-cartésien* (Paris, 1979).

Jean-Luc Marion, *Descartes: 'Règles utiles et claires pour la direction de l'esprit en la recherche de la vérité'* (The Hague, 1977).

Website

www.cartesius.net   Descartes E Il Seicento, maintained by Giulia Belgioioso (Director, Centro Interdipartmentali Di Studi Su Descartes E Il Seicento), Jean-Robert Armogathe (Centre d'Études cartésiennes), and their colleagues

Further Reading in Oxford World's Classics

Bacon, Francis, *The Essays or Counsels Civil and Moral*, ed. Brian Vickers.

Berkeley, George, *Principles of Human Knowledge and Three Dialogues*, ed. Howard Robinson.

A CHRONOLOGY OF RENÉ DESCARTES

1596   31 March: born at La Haye near Tours.

1607–15 Attends the Jesuit college of La Flèche.

1610   Galileo's observation of the four moons of Jupiter.

1616   Licenciate of Law, University of Poitiers.

1618   Joins the army of Prince Maurice of Nassau in Holland.

1619   Moves to the army of Elector Maximilian, duke of Bavaria, in Germany.

1619   10 November: dream of a 'wonderful science'.

1620   Publication of Bacon's *Novum Organum*.

1622–5 Travels in Europe.

1623–5 Imprisonment of Théophile de Viau as ringleader of the Parisian free-thinkers.

1625–8 Based in Paris, in the circle of Mersenne.

1628   Publication of Harvey's *Circulation of the Blood*.

1628 (or 1629) Completion of *Rules For the Direction of Our Native Intelligence*.

1628 (end) Move to Holland.

1629   Work on *The Universe*.

1633   Publication of Galileo's *Dialogue Concerning the Two Chief World Systems*.

1633   Condemnation of Galileo by the Roman Inquisition; Descartes abandons plans to publish *The Universe*.

1635   Birth of Descartes's natural daughter, named Francine, baptized 7 August (died 1640).

1637   Publication of *A Discourse on the Method*, with three essays: *Dioptrics*, *Meteorology*, and *Geometry*.

1641   Publication of *Meditations*, with the first six sets of Objections and Replies.

1642   Publication of second edition of *Meditations*, with all seven sets of Objections and Replies. First contact with Princess Elizabeth of Bohemia.

1643   Cartesian philosophy condemned at the University of Utrecht.

1644   Visit to France; publication of the Latin version of *The Principles of Philosophy* (French translation 1647), and the Latin version of the *Discourse* and the *Essays*.

1647   Award of a pension by the king of France; return to France to arrange its receipt. Publication of *Comments on a Certain Broadsheet*.

1648   16 April: interview with Frans Burman at Egmond-Binnen.

1648   Beginning of the civil war known as 'La Fronde' in France.

1649   Journey to Sweden on invitation of Queen Christina; publication of the *Passions of the Soul*.

1650   11 February: death in Stockholm from pneumonia.

1666   Descartes's remains returned to France, to rest eventually in Saint-Germain des Prés.

A DISCOURSE ON THE METHOD
OF CORRECTLY CONDUCTING
ONE'S REASON AND
SEEKING TRUTH IN THE SCIENCES

If this discourse seems too long to be read all at once,* it may
be split up into six parts. In the first will be found several
considerations relating to the sciences. In the second, the
principal rules of the method that the author has found. In the
third, some of the moral rules he has derived from this method.
In the fourth, the arguments by which he proves the existence
of God and of the human soul, which are the foundations of
his metaphysics. In the fifth, the order of the physical questions
he has investigated, and particularly the explanation of the
movement of the heart and some other problems pertaining to
medicine, as well as the difference between the human soul
and that of animals. And in the last part, the requirements he
believes are necessary to make progress beyond that which he
has already made in the study of nature, and the reasons that
prompted him to write.

PART ONE

Good sense* is the most evenly distributed thing in the world; for everyone believes himself to be so well provided with it that 2 even those who are the hardest to please in every other way do not usually want more of it than they already have. Nor is it likely that everyone is wrong about this; rather, what this shows is that the power of judging correctly and of distinguishing the true from the false (which is what is properly called good sense or reason) is naturally equal in all men, and that consequently the diversity of our opinions arises not from the fact that some of us are more reasonable than others, but solely that we have different ways of directing our thoughts, and do not take into account the same things. For it is not enough to possess a good mind; the most important thing is to apply it correctly.* The greatest minds are capable of the greatest vices as well as the greatest virtues; those who go forward but very slowly can get further, if they always follow the right road, than those who are in too much of a hurry and stray off it.*

For myself, I have never presumed my mind to be any way more accomplished than that of the common man. Indeed, I have often wished that my mind was as fast, my imagination as clear and precise, and my memory as well stocked and sharp as those of certain other people. And I personally know of no any other mental attributes that go to make up an accomplished mind;* for, as regards reason or good sense (insofar as it is the only thing that makes us human and distinguishes us from brute beasts), I am ready to believe that it is altogether complete in every one of us, and I am prepared to follow in this the agreed doctrine of those philosophers who say that differences of degree apply only to *accidents*, and not to *forms* or natures of 3 *individuals* of the same *species*.*

But I venture to claim that since my early youth I have had

the great good fortune of finding myself taking certain paths that have led me to reflections and maxims from which I have fashioned a method* by which, it seems to me, I have a way of adding progressively to my knowledge and raising it by degrees to the highest point that the limitations of my mind and the short span of life allotted to me will permit it to reach. For I have already reaped so many fruits from this method that I derive the highest satisfaction from the progress that I believe myself already to have made in my pursuit of truth, in spite of the fact that in appraising my own achievements I try always to err on the side of caution rather than that of presumption, and that when I cast a philosopher's eye over the various actions and undertakings of mankind, there is hardly a single one that does not seem to me to be vain and futile.* And I conceive such hopes for the future that if, among the purely human occupations,* there is one that is really good and important, I venture to believe that it is the one that I have chosen.

It is, however, possible that I am wrong, and that I am mistaking bits of copper and glass for gold and diamonds. I know how likely we are to be wrong on our own account, and how suspect is the judgement of our friends when it is in our favour. Nonetheless, in this essay I shall gladly reveal the paths I have followed and paint my life as it were in a picture, so that everyone may come to a judgement about it; and from hearing the reactions of the public to this picture,* I shall add a new way of acquiring knowledge to those which I habitually employ.

So my aim here is not to teach the method that everyone must follow for the right conduct of his reason, but only to show in what way I have tried to conduct mine.* Those who take it upon themselves to give direction to others must believe themselves more capable than those to whom they give it, and bear the responsibility for the slightest error they might make. But as I am putting this essay forward only as a historical record, or if you prefer, a fable, in which among a number of examples worthy of imitation one may also find several which one would be right not to follow, I hope that it may prove useful to some people without being harmful to any, and that my candour will be appreciated by everyone.

I was educated in classical studies* from my earliest years, and because I was given to believe that through them one could acquire clear and sure knowledge of everything that one needed in life, I was extremely eager to acquire them. But as soon as I had finished my course of study, at which time it is usual to be admitted to the ranks of the well educated, I completely changed my opinion, for I found myself bogged down in so many doubts and errors, that it seemed to me that having set out to become learned, I had derived no benefit from my studies, other than that of progressively revealing to myself how ignorant I was. And yet I was a pupil of one of the most 5 famous schools in Europe, in which I believed that there must be as learned men as are to be found anywhere on earth. There I had learnt everything that others were learning; and not just content with the subjects that we were taught, I had even read all the books that fell into my hands on subjects that are considered the most occult and recondite.* Moreover, I knew what assessment others had made of me, and realized that I was not thought inferior to my fellow pupils, even though several among them had already been singled out to take the place of our teachers. And finally, our age seemed to me to be as flourishing as any preceding age, and to abound in as many great minds. This emboldened me to judge all others by myself, and to think that there was no body of knowledge on earth that lived up to the expectations I had been given of it.

I did not, however, cease to hold the school curriculum in esteem. I know that the Greek and Latin that are taught there are necessary for understanding the writings of the ancients; that fables stimulate the mind through their charm; that the memorable deeds recorded in histories uplift it, and they help form our judgement when read in a discerning way; that reading good books is like engaging in conversation with the most

cultivated minds of past centuries who had composed them, or rather, taking part in a well-conducted dialogue in which such minds reveal to us only the best of their thoughts; that oratory is incomparably powerful and beautiful, and that poetry pos-
6 sesses delightful delicacy and charm;* that mathematics has very subtle techniques that can be of great use in satisfying curious minds, as well as in coming to the aid of all the arts, and reducing human labour; that books on morals contain highly instructive teachings and exhortations to virtue;* that theology charts our path to heaven; that philosophy provides us with the means of speaking *plausibly* about anything and impressing those who are less well instructed; that law, medicine, and other disciplines bring to those who profess them riches and honours;* and finally, that it is worthwhile to have studied all of these branches of knowledge, even the most superstitious and false, in order to learn their true value and avoid being deceived by them.

But I then decided that I had devoted enough time both to the study of languages and to the reading of the books, histories, and fables of the classical world. For conversing with those of another age is more or less the same thing as travelling. It is good to know something of the customs of different peoples in order to be able to judge our own more securely, and to prevent ourselves from thinking that everything not in accordance with our own customs is ridiculous and irrational, as those who have see nothing of the world are in the habit of doing. On the other hand, when we spend too much time travelling, we end up becoming strangers in our own country; and when we immerse ourselves too deeply in the practices of bygone ages, we usually remain woefully ignorant of the practices of our
7 own time. Moreover, fables make us conceive of events as being possible where they are not; and even if the most faithful of accounts of the past neither alter nor exaggerate the importance of things in order to make them more attractive to the reader, they nearly always leave out the humblest and least illustrious historical circumstances, with the result that what

8

remains does not appear as it really was, and that those who base their behaviour on the examples they draw from such accounts are likely to try to match the feats of knights of old* in tales of chivalry and set themselves targets beyond their powers.

I held oratory in high esteem, and loved poetry, but I looked upon both as gifts of the mind rather than fruits of study. Those who reason most powerfully and are the most successful at ordering their thoughts so as to make them clear and intelligible will always be best able to persuade others of what they say, even if they speak in the thickest of dialects* and have never learned any rhetoric. And those whose linguistic expression is the most pleasing and who frame their thoughts in the most eloquent and agreeable way would always end up being the best poets, even if they did not know a single rule of poetic composition.

I was most keen on mathematics, because of its certainty and the *incontrovertibility** of its proofs; but I did not yet see its true use. Believing as I did that its only application was to the mechanical arts,* I was astonished that nothing more exalted had been built on such sure and solid foundations; whereas, on the other hand, I compared the moral works of ancient pagan writers to splendid and magnificent palaces built on nothing 8 more than sand and mud. They exalt the virtues, and make them seem more worthy of esteem than anything else on earth; but they do not give sufficient indication of how to learn about them; and what they call by such a fine name is in many cases no more than lack of human feeling, pride, despair, or parricide.*

I revered our theology and hoped as much as anyone to reach heaven; but having learnt as an established fact that the path to heaven is as open to the most ignorant as to the most learned, and that the revealed truths that lead there are beyond our understanding, I would not have dared submit them to my own puny reasoning powers, and believed that in order to engage in the task of studying them, it was indispensable to have some extraordinary assistance from heaven, and to be more than merely human.*

I shall not say anything about philosophy except that, when I realized that it had been cultivated by the best minds for many centuries, and that nevertheless there is nothing in it that is not disputed and consequently is not subject to doubt, I was not so presumptuous as to hope to succeed better than others; and that seeing how different learned men may defend different opinions on the same subject, without there ever being more than one which is true, I deemed anything that was no more than *plausible** to be tantamount to false.

As for the other disciplines, in so far as they borrow their principles from philosophy, I concluded that nothing solid could have been built on such shaky foundations. Nor was the honour and the profit they held in prospect enough to persuade me to study them; for I considered myself, through the favour of providence, as not being in the position of having to earn my living from a learned profession for the betterment of my fortune; and although I did not go about sneering at worldly glory as is the habit of Cynics,* I nonetheless held that sort of glory, to which I could never hope to have a true claim, in low esteem. Finally, as for the low sciences,* I felt that I already knew well enough what they were worth to avoid falling for any of the promises of an alchemist, the predictions of an astrologer, the impostures of a magician, or the tricks and boasts of those who profess to know more than they do.

That is why, as soon as I reached an age that allowed me to escape from the control of my teachers, I abandoned altogether the study of letters. And having decided to pursue only that knowledge which I might find in myself or in the great book of the world, I spent the rest of my youth travelling, visiting courts and armies, mixing with people of different character and rank, accumulating different experiences, putting myself to the test in situations in which I found myself by chance, and at all times giving due reflection to things as they presented themselves to me so as to derive some benefit from them. For it seemed to me that I could discover much more truth from the reasoning that we all make about things that affect us and that will soon cause us harm if we misjudge them, than from the speculations in which a scholar engages in the privacy of his study, that have no consequence for him except insofar as the further they are from common sense, the more he will be proud of them, because he has had to use so much more ingenuity and subtlety in the struggle to make them *plausible*. And I constantly felt a burning desire to learn to distinguish the true from the false, to see my actions for what they were, and to proceed with confidence through life.

It is true that while I was thinking about the customs of other men and nothing else, I found little to provide me with certain knowledge; I observed in them as much diversity as I had found earlier among the opinions of the philosophers. And so the greatest benefit I derived from these observations was that when I was confronted by things which, although they seem to us very extravagant and ridiculous, are nevertheless widely accepted and approved of by other great nations, I learned not to believe too firmly in anything that only example and custom had persuaded me of.* So it was that I freed myself gradually from many of the errors that can obscure the natural light of our minds, and make them less able to see reason. But after having spent several years studying the book of the world and trying to acquire some experience of life, I took the decision one day to look into myself and to use all my mental powers to choose the paths I should follow. In this it seems to me that I have had much more success than if I had never left either my country or my books.

PART TWO

At that time I was in Germany, where I had been called by the wars that have not yet come to an end there; as I was returning to the army from the coronation of the emperor, I was halted by the onset of winter in quarters where, having no diverting company and fortunately also no cares or emotional turmoil* to trouble me, I spent the whole day shut up in a small room heated by a stove, in which I could converse with my own thoughts at leisure.* Among the first of these was the realization that things made up of different elements and produced by the hands of several master craftsmen are often less perfect than those on which only one person has worked. This is the case with buildings which a single architect has planned and completed, that are usually more beautiful and better designed than those that several architects have tried to patch together, using old walls that had been constructed for other purposes. This is also the case with those ancient cities, that in the beginning were no more than villages and have become, through the passage of time, great conurbations; when compared to orderly towns that an engineer designs without constraints on an empty plain,* they are usually so badly laid out that, even though their buildings viewed separately often display as much if not more artistic merit as those of orderly towns, yet if one takes into consideration the way they are disposed, a tall one here, a low one there, and the way they 12 cause the streets to wind and change level, they look more like the product of chance than of the will of men applying their reason. And if one considers further that there have always been officials whose task it was to ensure that the design of private buildings should contribute to the beauty of the town as a whole, it will become clear how difficult it is to carry anything through to completion when working only with what others have produced. This led me to the view that those nations who were once half-savage and only gradually became more civilized, and whose legislation was forced on them by acts of criminal mischief and legal disagreements, could not be as well governed as those which, from the first moment of their coming together as a nation, observed the constitution laid down by a prudent lawgiver; in the same way, it cannot be doubted that a state which has embraced the true religion whose laws God alone has made must be incomparably better governed than any other. To return to human affairs, I believe that if Sparta once flourished greatly, it was not because of the particular excellence of each one of its laws (seeing that many were very strange and even contrary to good morals*), but because having all been laid down by one man,* they were all directed to a single end. And so I came to believe that book-learning, or at least learning whose rational foundations are no better than *generally approved*, and which contains no real proof, is not as close to the truth, composed as it is of the opinions of many different people, as the simple reasoning that any man of good sense can produce about things in his pur- 13 view. And so, although I came to believe that, because we were children before we were men, and because for a long time we were governed by our appetites and our teachers (the former being often in conflict with the latter, with neither giving the best advice in every case), it is almost impossible that our judgements are as pure or as solid as they might have been if we had had full use of our reason from the moment of our birth, and had been guided by that alone.*

Admittedly, we do not see people pulling down all the houses of a town for the sole purpose of reconstructing them differently in order to embellish the streets; but we do see many people having their own houses demolished in order to rebuild them, and may note that they are even sometimes forced to do so when the buildings are in danger of falling down of themselves or their foundations are insecure. This example convinced me that it would not be reasonable for an individual to set out to reform a state by changing everything

from the foundations up, and overthrowing it in order to rebuild it, or even to set out to reform the body of knowledge or the established order in schools for teaching it;* but rather, as far as all the opinions I had hitherto accepted were concerned, I could do no better than to set about ridding myself of them once and for all, with a view to replacing them afterwards
14 either with better ones, or even the same ones, once I had tested them with my reason and ensured that they were set straight. I firmly believed that by these means I would manage to order my life better than if I built on old foundations and relied only upon old principles which had been inculcated in me when young, without my ever having sought to find out whether they were true. For although I could see a number of difficulties in all this, they were not unsurmountable; nor did they compare with those which are found in the smallest reform affecting the body public. Such a great body is too hard to rebuild if once destroyed, or even to keep standing if once shaken, and its fall cannot be anything other than very heavy. Moreover, as for any imperfections such bodies may have (and their very diversity is sufficient to ensure that some at least will have imperfections), custom may have considerably attenuated them, and even managed to circumvent or imperceptibly to correct many that could not have been so well remedied through the exercise of political judgement.* Finally, these imperfections are nearly all more bearable than change, in the same way that highways that wind their way between mountains become in the end so smooth and easy through use that it is much better to follow them than to attempt to seek a straighter path, by climbing over rocky promontories and plunging down into deep valleys.

That is why I could not possibly approve of those meddlesome and restless spirits who are called neither by birth nor by riches to take part in public affairs, yet are forever plotting some reform. And if I thought that there was anything what-
15 soever in this essay that could lead me to be suspected of the same folly, I should be very loath to allow it to be published.

My project has never extended beyond wishing to reform my own thoughts and build on a foundation which is mine alone. And if my work has pleased me enough for me to reveal to you here what it is based on, I do not want for all that to suggest that anyone should copy it. Those on whom God has bestowed His grace in greater measure will perhaps have more lofty designs;* but I very much fear that mine may already be too bold for many. Even the decision to rid oneself of all the opinions one has hitherto accepted is not an example which everyone ought to follow. The world is made up almost entirely of two sorts of minds to which such a course of action is wholly unsuitable. First, there are those who, believing themselves cleverer than they are, cannot stop themselves jumping to conclusions, and do not have enough patience to govern their thoughts in an orderly way, with the result that once they have allowed themselves to doubt accepted principles and stray from the common path, they would never be able to keep to the road that one must take to proceed in the right direction, and would remain lost all their lives. Second, there are those who, having enough sense or modesty to realize that they are less capable of distinguishing the true from the false than certain others by whom they could be guided, must content themselves with following the opinions of these others rather than seeking better ones from themselves.*

As for myself, I would perhaps have been in this second 16 category if I had only had one teacher, or if I had not known about the differences of opinion that have always existed among the most learned. But having already discovered at school that there is no opinion so bizarre and incredible that has not been uttered by some philosopher or other,* and having come later in the course of my travels to the realization that all those who have opinions that are diametrically opposed to ours are not on that account barbarians or savages, but that among their number there are many who make use of their reason as much or more than we do; and having considered how a given man with a given mind, brought up since childhood among the French or the Germans, develops differently from the way he would if he had always lived among the Chinese or among cannibals, and how even down to our fashion of dress, the very thing that pleased us ten years ago and may perhaps please us in ten years' time at present seems outlandish and ridiculous to our eyes (this is because we are much more swayed by custom and example than any certain knowledge; and yet the *majority view** is of no value as proof of truths which are difficult to discover, because they are much more likely to be discovered by one man by himself than by a whole people); for all these reasons, I could not choose any one person whose opinions struck me as preferable to those of others, and I found myself forced, as it were, to provide for myself my own guidance.

But like a man walking by himself in the dark, I took the
17 decision to go so slowly and to exercise such caution in everything that even if I made very little progress, I would at least be sure not to fall. I did not even wish to begin by rejecting absolutely all the opinions that might have slipped into my mind without having been introduced there by reason, until I had first spent enough time planning the work I was undertaking and searching for the true method of arriving at the knowledge of everything that my mind was capable of grasping.

In earlier years I had made some study of logic in the philosophy course, and of geometrical analysis and algebra in mathematics, three arts or branches of knowledge that seemed destined to contribute to my plan. But, on examining them, I noted, in the case of logic, that its syllogisms and most of its other techniques are employed more to explain things to other people that one knows already or even, as in the art of Lull, to speak injudiciously about those of which one is ignorant, than to learn anything new.* And although logic really does contain many very true and excellent precepts, there are so many others mixed in with them that are either harmful or superfluous, that it is almost as difficult to separate the former from the latter as it is to extract a statue of Diana or Minerva from a

rough block of marble.* As for ancient geometrical analysis and modern algebra, even apart from the fact that they deal only in highly abstract matters that seem to have no practical application, the former is so closely tied to the consideration of figures that it is unable to exercise the intellect without greatly   18
tiring the imagination, while in the latter case one is so much a slave to certain rules and symbols that it has been turned into a confused and obscure art that bewilders the mind instead of being a form of knowledge that cultivates it.* This was why I thought that another method had to be found which retained the advantages of all three but was free from their defects. And just as a great number of laws is often a pretext for wrong-doing, with the result that a state is much better governed when, having only a few, they are strictly observed; so also I came to believe that in the place of the great number of pre-cepts that go to make up logic, the following four would be sufficient for my purposes, provided that I took a firm and unshakeable decision never once to depart from them.

The first was never to accept anything as true that I did not *incontrovertibly* know to be so; that is to say, carefully to avoid both *prejudice* and premature conclusions; and to include nothing in my judgements other than that which presented itself to my mind so *clearly* and *distinctly*, that I would have no occasion to doubt it.*

The second was to divide all the difficulties under examination into as many parts as possible, and as many as were required to solve them in the best way.

The third was to conduct my thoughts in a given order, beginning with the *simplest* and most easily understood objects, and gradually ascending, as it were step by step, to the knowledge of the most *complex*; and *positing** an order even on those which do not have a natural order of precedence.*   19

The last was to undertake such complete enumerations and such general surveys that I would be sure to have left nothing out.*

The long chains of reasonings, every one simple and easy,

which geometers habitually employ to reach their most difficult proofs had given me cause to suppose that all those things which fall within the domain of human understanding follow on from each other in the same way, and that as long as one stops oneself taking anything to be true that is not true and sticks to the right order so as to deduce one thing from another, there can be nothing so remote that one cannot eventually reach it, nor so hidden that one cannot discover it.* And I had little difficulty in determining those with which it was necessary to begin, for I already knew that I had to begin with the simplest and the easiest to understand; and considering that of all those who had up to now sought truth in the sphere of human knowledge, only mathematicians have been able to discover any proofs, that is, any certain and *incontrovertible* arguments, I did not doubt that I should begin as they had done. Nor did I expect any other usefulness from this, than to accustom my mind to nourish itself on truths and reject false reasonings. Yet I did not, for all that, intend to study all those particular branches of knowledge which habitually go under the name of mathematics;* I saw that, although their objects were different, they nevertheless all concurred insofar as they only took into consideration the different relations or proportions to be found among these objects, and I came to think that it was best for me to examine only these proportions in general,* without *supposing* their existence except in those areas of enquiry which would serve to make my knowledge of them easier; and moreover, not to restrict them to those areas, in order to be better able to apply them thereafter to everything else to which they might be applied. Then, having noted that, in order to know them, I would sometimes need to think about them separately, and sometimes only bear them in mind, or consider many together, I came to the view that, in order to consider these proportions best separately, I had to suppose them to hold between lines, because I found nothing simpler nor more capable of being distinctly represented to my imagination* and to my senses. But for the purpose of retaining them in my memory, or grasping several together, it was necessary for me to designate them by the briefest possible symbols;* by this means I would borrow what was best from geometrical analysis and algebra, and would correct all the defects of the one by the other.

And indeed, I venture to claim that the scrupulous observance of the few precepts I had chosen gave me such ease in unravelling all the questions covered by these two branches of knowledge that in the two or three months I spent investigating them,* having begun with the simplest and most general (every truth that I discovered being a rule that I used 21 afterwards to find others), not only did I solve some which I had earlier judged very difficult, but it also seemed to me, towards the end of this period, that I was able to determine, even in respect of those questions which I had not solved, by what means and to what extent it was possible to solve them. In claiming this I will appear perhaps less conceited to you if you consider that, as there is only one truth of any one thing, whoever finds it knows as much as can be known about it, and that, for example, a child trained in arithmetic who does a sum according to the rules can be quite certain of having discovered everything the human mind can find out about the sum in question. In short, the method that teaches one to follow the correct order and to enumerate all the factors of the object under examination, contains everything that confers certainty on arithmetical rules.

But what pleased me most about this method was that, through it, I was certain in all cases to employ my reason, if not perfectly, then at least to the best of my ability; moreover, I believed that, in practising it, my mind was gradually getting used to conceiving of its objects more clearly and distinctly, and that not having set it to work on any particular matter, I was able to set myself the task of applying it just as usefully to the problems of other branches of knowledge* as I had done to those of algebra. Not that I ventured, for all that, to examine all the problems I might come across; for that would have been

contrary to the order prescribed by my method. But having noted that the principles of each branch of knowledge must of
22 necessity all be borrowed from philosophy, in which I could still find no certain principles, I came to think that it was first necessary for me to try to establish some; and that this being the most important thing in the world and one in which undue haste and preconceptions were most to be feared, I thought that I ought not to attempt to carry this task through to completion until I had reached a much more mature age than the twenty-three years I then was, and until I had spent considerable time in preparing myself for the task, as much by rooting out of my mind all the false opinions I had accepted up to then, as by amassing a large number of experiences to serve afterwards as the matter of my reasoning, and by continually practising my chosen method in order to strengthen my grasp of it.

PART THREE

Finally, just as it is not enough, before beginning to rebuild the house in which one lives, to do no more than demolish it, make provision for materials and architects, or become oneself trained as an architect, or even to have carefully drawn up the plans, but one must also provide oneself with another house in which one may be comfortably lodged while work is in progress; so also, in order not to remain indecisive in my actions while my reason was forcing me to be so in my judgements, and to carry on living from then on as happily as I could, I formed a provisional moral code* for myself consisting in only three or four maxims, which I should like to share with you.

The first was to obey the laws and customs of my country,* 23 and to adhere to the religion in which God by His grace had me instructed from my childhood, and to govern myself in everything else according to the most moderate and least extreme opinions, being those commonly received among the *wisest* of those with whom I should have to live. For, having begun already to discount my own opinions because I wished to subject them all to rigorous examination, I was certain that I could do no better than to follow those of the wisest. And although there may be as many wise people among the Persians and the Chinese as among ourselves, it seemed to me that the most useful thing to do would be to regulate my conduct by that of the people among whom I was to live; and that for me to know what their opinions really were, I had to take note of what they did rather than what they said,* not only because in the present corrupt state of our morals few people are willing to declare everything they believe, but also because some do not even know what they believe; for the mental act by which we believe something, being different from that act by which we know that we believe it,* often results in one act being present without the other. And I chose only the most moderate among many opinions which were equally widely received, as much because these are always easiest to practise and likely to be the best (excesses all being usually bad) as to wander less far from the true path in case I should be wrong, and that having followed one extreme, it transpired that I should have followed 24 the other. And in particular, I placed in the category of these excesses all personal commitments by which one relinquishes some of one's freedom. Not that I disapprove of the laws that, in order to counteract the inconsistency of those who are weak-minded, permit men to make verbal undertakings or contracts which bind them not to break them (in cases where they have some worthy plan, or even, to guarantee the security of commerce, some plan which is no more than morally indifferent); but, because I saw nothing in this world which remained always in the same state, and because in my own case I set myself the task of gradually perfecting my judgements and not of making them worse, I would have seen myself as sinning against good sense if, having once approved of something, I should have found myself obliged to take it to be good later on, when it might have ceased to be so, or I might have ceased to consider it so.

My second maxim was to be as firm and resolute in my actions as I could, and to follow no less constantly the most doubtful opinions, once I had opted for them, than I would have if they had been the most certain ones.* In this I imitated those travellers who, finding themselves lost in a forest, must not wander in circles first to one side then to the other, and still less stop in one place, but have to walk as straight as possible in one direction, and not alter course for weak reasons, even if it might only have been chance which had led them to settle on the direction they had chosen; for by this means, even if they do not end up precisely where they want to be, they will even-
25 tually reach somewhere where they will most likely be better off than the middle of a forest. And, in the same way, as in life we must often act without delay, it is a very certain truth that when it is not in our power to determine which the truest

opinions are, we should follow those which are most likely to be true, and even though we might see no more *probability** in some rather than others, we must nevertheless opt for one set, and thereafter consider them not as being doubtful, insofar as they relate to the practice of life, but as altogether true and certain, because the reasoning that led us to opt for them is true and certain. This maxim was able from then on to free me from all the regret and remorse that usually troubles the consciences of weak and vacillating minds, who are inconsistent and allow themselves to follow certain practices as though they were good, that they later judge to be bad.

My third maxim was to endeavour always to master myself rather than fortune, to try to change my desires rather than to change the order of the world, and in general to settle for the belief that there is nothing entirely in our power except our thoughts, and after we have tried, in respect of things external to us, to do our best, everything in which we do not succeed is absolutely impossible as far as we are concerned.* This alone seemed to me to be sufficient to prevent me from desiring anything in future which I could not obtain, and thereby to make me content. For as our will is naturally inclined to desire 26 only those things which our intellect represents to it as possible in some way, it is certain that if we consider all external goods as being equally beyond our power, we shall not feel any more regret at failing to obtain those which seem to be our birthright when deprived of them through no fault of our own, than we shall for not possessing the kingdoms of China and Mexico; and by making a virtue out of necessity, as the saying goes, we shall no more desire to be healthy when we are ill or free when we are in prison, than we do now to have bodies made of matter as incorruptible as diamonds or wings to allow us to fly like birds. But I admit that it takes long practice and reiterated periods of meditation* to make oneself used to seeing things from this angle; and I believe that it is principally in this that lay the secret of those philosophers who were able in earlier times to escape the tyranny of fortune and, in spite of suffering and poverty, to rival their gods in happiness.* For through constant reflection on the limits laid upon them by nature, they convinced themselves so completely that nothing was in their power other than their thoughts, that this conviction alone was sufficient to prevent them from having any desire for anything else; and they controlled their thoughts so effectively that they thereby believed themselves with some reason to be richer, more powerful, freer, and happier than any 27 other men who, not having this philosophy, never have this control over their desires, however favoured by nature and fortune they may be.*

Finally, as a conclusion to this moral code, I decided to review the various occupations that men have in this life, in order to try to select the best one. Without wishing to pass judgement on the occupations of others, I came to the view that I could do no better than to continue in the one in which I found myself, that is to say, to devote my life to the cultivation of my reason and make such progress as I could in the knowledge of the truth following the method I had prescribed for myself. I had experienced such great joy since I began to employ this method that I did not believe that any sweeter or more innocent pleasures were to be had in this life; and as I discovered daily by its means a number of truths that seemed to me very important and generally unknown to other men, the satisfaction that I obtained from it filled my mind to such a degree that nothing else mattered to me. Besides, the three foregoing maxims were based only on the plan I had to continue to seek knowledge; for since God has given each of us an inner light* to distinguish the true from the false, I would not have believed for one moment that I should content myself with the opinions of others, if I had not intended in due course to use my own judgement to examine them; and I could not have avoided having scruples about following them, if I had not hoped thereby to seize every opportunity to find better 28 ones, in case there were any. Finally, I should not have known how to limit my desires or achieve happiness, if I had not followed a path by which I thought I was sure to acquire all the knowledge of which I was capable, and, by the same means, all the true goods that it would ever be in my power to obtain; and seeing that our will tends to pursue or shun only what our intellect represents to it as good or bad, it is sufficient to make a sound judgement in order to act well, and to judge as well as we can in order to do our best;* that is to say, to acquire all the virtues and with them all the other goods we are capable of acquiring. And when we are certain that this state of affairs exists, we cannot fail to be happy.

Once I had established these maxims, and set them aside in my mind with the truths of the faith which have always held first place in my beliefs, I took the decision that, as far as the rest of my opinions were concerned, I could freely undertake to rid myself of them. And seeing that I expected to be better able to complete this task in the company of others than by remaining shut any longer in the stove-heated room in which I had had all these thoughts, I set out on my travels again before winter was over. And through all the next nine years* I did nothing but wander through the world, trying to be a spectator rather than an actor in all the dramas that are played out on that stage; and, reflecting particularly in each matter on what might make it suspect and give occasion for error, I proceeded to eradicate from my mind all the mistakes that might earlier 29 have crept into it. In doing this, I was not copying those sceptics who doubt for doubting's sake, and pretend to be always unable to reach a decision;* for, on the contrary, the aim of my whole plan was to reach certainty and reject shifting ground in the search for rock and clay. And in this, it seems to me, I succeeded reasonably well, seeing that, in trying to expose the falsity or uncertainty of the propositions that I was investigating not by weak conjectures but by clear and certain reasoning, I found none so doubtful that I could not draw some reasonably certain conclusion from it, even if the conclusion was no more than that the proposition in question contained nothing of certainty. And just as, in demolishing an old building, one usually preserves the debris in order to use it in constructing a new one; so also, in destroying all those of my opinions which I judged to be ill-founded, I made various observations and accumulated many experiences* which have been of use to me subsequently in establishing more certain opinions. What is more, I continued to practise the method I had prescribed for myself, for, besides taking care generally to conduct all my thoughts according to these rules, I occasionally set aside a few hours which I spent applying it to difficulties in mathematics, or even to others which I could more or less translate into mathematical terms by removing from them all the principles of the other branches of knowledge which I did not find solid enough; you will see I have done this to many problems that are dealt with in this volume.* And so, while apparently living in the same way as those who, having no occupation other than leading a blameless and agreeable life, take care to keep their pleasures free from vices and who, in order to enjoy their leisure without becoming bored, engage in all those pastimes that are honourable, I never stopped pursuing my plan and making progress in the knowledge of truth, perhaps more than if I had done nothing else than read books* and spend time in the company of men of letters.

However, those nine years passed by before I had reached any decision about the questions that are often debated among the learned, or had begun to look for the foundations of any philosophy which might be more certain than that which is commonly received. And the example of the many excellent minds who, having embarked on this project before me, did not appear to have succeeded,* led me to see it as so difficult that I would perhaps not have dared to undertake the task so early if I had not learned that some people were already spreading the rumour that I had completed it. I cannot say on what they based this opinion. If I have done anything to contribute to it by what I have said in public, it must have been by owning up to what I did not know with greater freedom than is usual among those who have undertaken some study, and perhaps also by revealing the reasons that I had to doubt much that others take to be certain, rather than by boasting of any positive knowledge. But having enough self-esteem not to wish to be taken for other than I was, I came to think that it was necessary for me to try by every possible means to make myself worthy of the reputation I was being given. And it is now just eight years since this desire made me decide to move away from all the places where I might have acquaintances and to retire here,* in a country in which the long period of war has established such good discipline that the armies that are maintained here seem only to serve to ensure that people enjoy the fruits of peace with correspondingly greater security, and where amid a teeming, active, great people that shows more interest in its own affairs than curiosity for those of others, I have been able to live as solitary and as retiring a life as I would in the most remote of deserts, while lacking none of the comforts found in the most populous cities.*

31

PART FOUR

I do not know whether I am bound to tell you about the first meditations that I engaged in there, for they are so metaphysical and recondite that they may not be to everyone's taste. And yet, to make it possible to judge whether the foundations I have laid are firm enough, I find myself in a way forced to speak about them. As has already been said, I had long since observed that, as far as morals are concerned, it is necessary sometimes to follow opinions which one knows to be very unsure as if they were indubitable; but because I wished at that time to concentrate on the pursuit of truth, I came to think that I should do the exact opposite and reject as completely false everything in which I could detect the least doubt, in order to see if anything thereafter remained in my belief that was completely indubitable. And so, because our senses sometimes deceive us, I decided to suppose that nothing was such as they lead us to imagine it to be.* And because there are men who make mistakes in reasoning, even about the simplest elements of geometry, and commit logical fallacies, I judged that I was as prone to error as anyone else, and I rejected as false all the reasoning I had hitherto accepted as valid proof.* Finally, considering that all the same thoughts which we have while awake can come to us while asleep without any one of them then being true, I resolved to pretend that everything that had ever entered my head was no more true than the illusions of my dreams. But immediately afterwards I noted that, while I was trying to think of all things being false in this way, it was necessarily the case that I, who was thinking them, had to be something; and observing this truth: *I am thinking therefore I exist*,* was so secure and certain* that it could not be shaken by any of the most extravagant suppositions of the sceptics, I judged that I could accept it without scruple, as the first principle of the philosophy I was seeking.*

32

28

Next, examining attentively what I was, I saw that I could pretend that I had no body and that there was no world or place for me to be in, but that I could not for all that pretend that I did not exist; on the contrary, from the very fact that I thought of doubting the truth of other things, it followed *incontrovertibly* and certainly that I myself existed, whereas, if I had merely ceased thinking, I would have no reason to believe 33 that I existed, even if everything else I had ever imagined had been true. I thereby concluded that I was a *substance* whose whole *essence* or nature resides only in thinking, and which, in order to exist, has no need of place and is not dependent on any material thing. Accordingly this 'I', that is to say, the Soul* by which I am what I am, is entirely distinct from the body and is even easier to know than the body; and would not stop being everything it is, even if the body were not to exist.

After this, I came to think in general about what is required for a proposition to be true and certain; for since I had just found one such proposition, I thought that I ought also to know in what this certainty consists. And having observed that there was nothing in this proposition, *I am thinking therefore I exist*, which makes me sure that I am telling the truth, except that I can see very clearly that, in order to think, one has to exist, I concluded that I could take it to be a general rule that things we conceive of very clearly and distinctly are all true, but that there is some difficulty in being able to identify those which we conceive of distinctly.

As a result of which, as I thought about the fact that I was doubting and that consequently my being was not altogether perfect (for I saw clearly that it was a greater perfection to know than to doubt), I decided to look for the source from which I had learned to think of something more perfect than I was myself, and I came to the *incontrovertible* realization that this must be from some nature that was in fact more perfect. 34 As for the thoughts I had about many other things outside myself, such as the heavens, the earth, light, heat, and numerous others, I had no such difficulty in knowing where they came from, because, seeing nothing in them which seemed to make them superior to myself, I could believe that if they were true, they depended on my nature in so far as it contained some perfection; and if they were not true, I held them from nothing, that is to say, that they were in me because I was lacking something.* But this could not be true of the idea of a being more perfect than mine; for it was manifestly impossible that I should hold this from nothing; and because it is no less contradictory that the more perfect should proceed from and depend on the less perfect than it is that something should proceed from nothing,* I could not hold it from myself either. So that there remained only the possibility that it had been put into me by a nature which was truly more perfect than mine, and one which even had in itself all the perfections of which I could have any idea, that is to say, in a word, which was God.* To which thought I added that, because I knew some perfections that I did not myself have, I was not the only being who existed (I shall here freely employ, with your permission, some scholastic terminology), but that *of necessity* there must be some other, more perfect being upon whom I depended and from whom I had acquired all that I possessed. For if I had been the sole being and had been independent of every other

35 being so as to *have*, *of myself*, that small degree of *participation* in the perfection which I shared with the perfect being, I could have been able to *have of myself*, by the same reason, all the remaining perfection that I knew myself to lack,* and so be myself infinite, eternal, unchanging, omniscient, in a word, to have all the perfections which I could observe in God. For, by following this line of reasoning, for me to know the nature of God in so far as my own nature permitted it, I only had to consider, in respect of each thing of which I found in myself some idea, whether it was a perfection to possess it; and I was certain that none of those things which manifested any imperfection was in Him, but that all the others were. In this way I could see that doubt, inconstancy, sadness, and such things could not be in Him, given that I would have been myself very

glad to be free of them. Besides this, I had ideas of many corporeal things in the realm of the sensory; for even if I were to *suppose* that I was dreaming and that everything that I saw or imagined was false, I nevertheless could not deny that the ideas were really in my thought; but because I had already recognized in my own case that the nature of the intellect is distinct from the nature of the body, and considering that all composition is evidence of dependence, and that dependence is manifestly a defect,* I concluded that it could not be one of God's perfections to be composed of these two natures, and that, as a consequence, He was not so composed; but that, if there were in the world any bodies or other intelligences* or other natures which were not wholly perfect, their being must depend on His power, in such a way that they could not continue to subsist for a single moment without Him.* 36

I decided after that to look for other truths; I called to mind the object of study of geometers, which I conceived of as a continuous body or a space indefinitely extended in length, breadth, and height or depth, divisible into different parts which could have various figures and sizes, and be moved or transposed in all sorts of ways, for geometers *posit* all that to be their object of study. I ran through some of their simpler proofs, and observed that the great certainty which everyone attributes to them is based only on the fact that they are conceived of as *incontrovertible*, following the rule that I have just given. I noted also that there was absolutely nothing in them which made me certain of the existence of their object. Thus, for example, I grasped clearly that, *supposing* a triangle to be given, it was necessary that its three angles were equal to two right angles; yet for all that, I saw nothing in this which made me certain that a single triangle existed in the world. Whereas, going back to the idea I had had of a perfect being, I found that existence was part of that idea, in the same way, or even more *incontrovertibly* so, that it is intrinsic to the idea of a triangle that its three angles equal two right angles, or to that of a sphere that all its parts are equidistant from its centre; and that, in consequence, it is at least as certain as any geometric proof that God, who is that perfect being, is or exists.*

37   But what convinces many people that there is a problem in knowing Him and even of knowing what their soul is, is that they never raise their mind above the realm of sensory things and are so used not to think of anything except by imagining it, which is a mode of thinking peculiar to material objects, that everything which seems unimaginable seems to them unintelligible.* This is clear enough from the fact that even scholastic philosophers hold as a maxim that there is nothing in the intellect which has not previously been in the senses,* in which, however, it is certain that the ideas of God and the soul have never been. It seems to me that people who wish to use their imagination in order to understand these ideas are doing the same as if, in order to hear sounds or smell smells, they tried to use their eyes. Except that there is this further difference, that the sense of sight no more confirms to us the reality of things than that of smell or hearing, whereas neither our imagination nor our senses could ever confirm the existence of anything, if our intellect did not play its part.

Finally, if there are still people who are not sufficiently convinced of the existence of God and of their soul by the arguments I have adduced, I would have them know that everything else of which they think they can be more certain, such as their having a body, or there being stars and an earth and suchlike, is in fact less certain. For although for all practical purposes we possess an assurance* of these things such

38   that it seems that no one can doubt their existence without being wilfully eccentric, nevertheless, where metaphysical certainty is in question, no one can deny, short of being irrational, that there are sufficient grounds for not being absolutely certain, as when we note that while we are asleep we can in the same way imagine having another body, or seeing other stars and another earth, without this being in fact the case. For how do we know that the thoughts that come to us in dreams are any more false than the others, seeing that they are often no

less vivid and clear? However much the best minds choose to
investigate this matter, I do not believe that they will be able to
furnish any argument which is sufficient to remove this doubt,
unless they presuppose the existence of God. For, in the first
place, even the rule which I stated above that I held—namely,
that the things that we conceive very clearly and very distinctly
are all true—is only certain because God is or exists, because
He is a perfect being, and because everything that is in us
comes from Him.* From which it follows that our ideas or
notions, being real things which moreover come from God,
insofar as they are clear and distinct, cannot thereby but be
true. So that if we quite often have ideas containing some
falsity, these can only be those which contain something in
some way confused or obscure, because in this they *participate*
in nothingness, that is to say, that they are in us in this confused form because we are not wholly perfect.* And it is manifest that there is no less contradiction in the proposition that
falsity and imperfection as such come from God, than there is 39
in the proposition that truth or perfection come from nothingness. But if we did not know that everything that is real and
true in us comes from a perfect and infinite being, then, no
matter how clear and distinct our ideas were, we would have no
reason to be assured that they possess the perfection of being
true.

Now once the knowledge of God and of the soul has made
us certain of this rule, it is a simple matter to determine that
the things we imagine in dreams should in no way make us
doubt the truth of the thoughts we have while awake. For even
if one should happen while sleeping to have some very distinct
idea, as for example, in the case of a geometer discovering
some new proof, the fact that he was asleep would not prevent
it being true. And as for the most common error of our
dreams, which consists in their representing various things to
us in the same way as our external senses, it does not matter
that it gives us occasion to distrust the truth of such ideas,
because our senses could also quite often mislead us without

our being asleep;* as when those who suffer from jaundice see everything as yellow, or when stars or other very distant bodies appear to us much smaller than they are. For after all, whether we are awake or asleep, we ought never to let ourselves be convinced except on the evidence of our reason. And it is to be noted that I say 'our reason', and not 'our imagination' or 'our senses'. For although we see the sun very clearly, we should not on that account judge that it is only as large as we see it; and we can well imagine the head of a lion grafted onto the body of a goat, without having necessarily to conclude from this that a chimera exists in the world;* for reason does not dictate to us that what we see or imagine in this way is true. But it does certainly dictate that all our ideas or notions must have some foundation in truth; for it would not otherwise be possible that God, who is all-perfect and altogether true, should have placed them in us unless it were so. Our processes of reasoning are never so clear or so complete while we are asleep as when we are awake (even though our imaginings in sleep are sometimes just as vivid and distinct); so reason tells us also that as our thoughts cannot all be true because we are not wholly perfect, what truth there is in them must infallibly* be found in those we have while awake rather than in those we have in our dreams.

PART FIVE

I would gladly go on and reveal the whole chain of the other truths that I deduced from these first ones. But in order to achieve this end, it would be necessary here for me to broach several questions that are controversial among learned men with whom I do not wish to fall out, and so I believe it would be best for me to abstain from doing this, and state only in broad terms what these questions are, in order to leave wiser heads to judge whether it would be profitable for the public to be informed about them in greater detail. I have always stuck 41 to the decision I took not to *posit* any principle other than that which I have just used to prove the existence of God and of the soul, and not to take anything to be true which did not seem to me clearer and more certain than the proofs of geometers had previously seemed. And yet I venture to say that I have not only found the way to satisfy myself in a short space of time about all the principal difficulties usually discussed in philosophy, but I have also come to see certain laws which God has established in such a way in nature, and of which He has imprinted notions of such a kind in our souls, that after sufficient reflection on them, we cannot doubt that they are strictly observed in everything that exists or occurs in the world. Moreover, by considering what follows from these laws, it seems to me that I have discovered many truths more useful and important than anything I had hitherto learned or even hoped to learn.

But since I tried to explain the most important of these in a treatise which certain considerations prevent me from publishing,* I cannot let them be known better than by saying here briefly what the treatise contains. Before I started writing it, I had intended to include in it everything that I believed I knew about the nature of material things. But just like those painters who, being unable to represent equally in a flat picture all the

35

various faces of a solid body, choose only one of the principal ones which they place in the light, leaving the others in shadow, representing them to the extent that one can see them when one looks at the chosen face; so also, fearing that I could not put everything that I had in my mind in my discourse, I undertook only to reveal fully my conception of light; thereafter, I took the opportunity of adding something about the sun and the fixed stars, because light proceeds almost wholly from them; something about the heavens, because they transmit it; something about the planets, the comets, and the earth, because they reflect it; and in particular something about terrestrial bodies, because they are either coloured, or transparent, or luminous; and finally something about man, because he is the spectator of all this. And in order to remove these things from the spotlight and to be able to say more freely what I thought about them without being obliged either to confirm or refute the opinions of learned men, I decided to leave this earth wholly for them to discuss, and to speak only of what would happen in a new world, if God were now to create enough matter to compose it somewhere in imaginary space,* and if He were to agitate the different parts of this matter in diverse and indiscriminate ways so as to create from it a chaos as confused as any poet could possibly imagine; and that He then did no more than sustain nature in His usual manner, leaving it to act according to the laws He has established. So I first described this matter and tried to represent it so that there is nothing in the world, I think, clearer and more intelligible, except what has just been said of God and the soul; for I even made the explicit *supposition* expressly that it contained none of the *forms* or *qualities** which are discussed by scholastic philosophers, and that it had nothing in general that was not so naturally known to our souls that we could not even pretend to be ignorant of it. Further, I revealed what were the laws of nature; and basing my reasoning on no other principle than the infinite perfections of God, I set out to prove all those laws about which one might have had some doubt, and to show that they are such that even if God had created many worlds, there could be not be any in which they could have failed to be observed. After that, I demonstrated how the greater part of the matter of this chaos must, in consequence of these laws, be disposed and arranged in a way which made it similar to the heavens above us; how, at the same time, some of its parts had to compose an earth, some others planets and comets, yet others a sun and fixed stars. And here, enlarging on the subject of light,* I explained in detail the nature of the light to be found in the sun and the heavenly bodies, the way it crossed in an instant the immense expanses of the heavens, and how it was reflected from the planets and the comets towards the earth. I added also many things about the *substance*, position, motions, and all the various *qualities* of these heavens and stars; so that I thought I had said enough to show that nothing was to be observed in those of our world which must not or at least could not appear wholly similar to the world I was describing. Next, 44 I came to speak about the earth in particular, and to discuss how, although I had made the explicit *supposition* that God conferred no weight* on the matter of which it was composed, all its parts nonetheless tended exactly towards its centre; how, there being water and air on its surface, the dispositions of the heavens and the heavenly bodies (principally the moon) must cause tidal movement similar in every circumstance to that which we observe in our seas; and together with all this, a certain current, as much of the water as of the air, from east to west, such as we find here in our tropics; how mountains, seas, springs, and rivers could naturally form themselves, metals appear in the mines, plants grow in the countryside, and in general, how all the bodies that are called *mixed* or *composed* come into being there. And among other things, because apart from the heavenly bodies I knew of nothing in the world which produces light apart from fire, I set out to explain very clearly everything which pertains to its nature, how it comes about and how it sustains itself; how there is sometimes only heat without light and sometimes only light without heat; how it

37

can introduce different colours and various other *qualities* into different bodies; how it melts some things and hardens others, how it can consume nearly all of them or turn them into ashes and smoke; and finally, how it can form glass from these ashes, by nothing other than the power of its action. I took particular
45 pleasure in describing this, for the transmutation of ashes into glass seemed to me as remarkable a transformation as any that occurs in nature.

Yet I did not wish to infer from all this that our world was created in the way I suggested; for it is much more *plausible* that from the beginning God made it as it was to be. But it is certain (and this is an opinion widely held among theologians) that the act by which He conserves the world is the same as that by which He created it.* So, even if He might not have given it any other form at the beginning than chaos, provided that He established the laws of nature and gave nature the help to act as it usually acts, we may believe, without casting doubt upon the miracle of creation,* that all purely material things would have been able, in time, to make themselves into what we see them to be at present in this way alone. And their nature is much easier to conceive of, when we think of their gradual emergence in this way, than when we only consider them in their final form.

From the description of inanimate bodies and plants I passed to that of animals, and in particular to that of men. But because I did not yet know enough to speak about it in the same way as I did about the rest, that is to say, by proving effects from causes, and showing from what elements and by what process nature must produce them, I contented myself with the *supposition* that God formed the body of a man,
46 exactly like our own both in the external shape of his members and in the internal configuration of his organs, constituting him of no other matter than that which I had already described, and without placing in him in the beginning a *rational* soul, or anything else which could function as a *vegetative* or *sensitive* soul,* but merely kindling in his heart one of

those fires without light which I had already explained and whose nature I conceived of as no different from the fire that heats hay when it has been stored before it was dry, or makes new wine rise in temperature, when it is left to ferment on the lees. For, in investigating the functions that could as a consequence be in this body, I found precisely all those which can be in us without our thinking of them, and to which our soul, that is to say, that part of us distinct from the body whose sole nature, as has been said above, is to think, contributes nothing; these functions are the same as those in which irrational animals may be said to resemble us. But I was unable to find in this body any of those functions which, being dependent on thought, are the only ones that belong to us as human beings, whereas I found them all there subsequently, once I had supposed that God created a *rational soul* and that He joined it to this body in a particular way which I described.

But so that one may see how I dealt with this matter, I wish to give here the explanation of the movement of the heart and the arteries, from which, being the first and most general movement that is observed in animals, readers will determine more easily what they must think about all the others. And so 47 that they might have less difficulty understanding what I shall say about it, I should like those who are unversed in anatomy to take the trouble, before reading this, of having the heart of a large animal with lungs dissected before their eyes (for it is in all respects sufficiently like that of a man) and of having its two chambers or cavities pointed out to them. First, the one which is on the right side, to which two very wide tubes are connected; that is, the *vena cava*, which is the principal receptacle of blood and, as it were, the trunk of the tree of which all other veins in the body are the branches; and the *vena arteriosa*, which has been ill-named, being in fact an artery, which has its origin in the heart, and having emerged from it, divides into many branches that spread throughout the lungs. Next, the cavity on the left side, to which two tubes are connected in the same way, which are as wide or wider than the preceding ones; that is, the *arteria venosa*, which has also been ill-named, because it is nothing other than a vein, which comes from the lungs where it is divided into many branches, intertwined with those of the *vena arteriosa*, and those with the tube called the *trachea* through which the air we breathe enters; and the *aorta* which, coming out from the heart, sends its branches throughout the body. I should also like my readers to be shown carefully the eleven small membranes which, like so many little doors, open and close the four apertures which are in these two

48 cavities; namely, three at the entrance to the *vena cava*, where they are so disposed that they cannot prevent the blood it contains from flowing into the right cavity of the heart and yet at the same time completely stop the blood from leaving it; three at the entrance to the *vena arteriosa*, which, being disposed in the opposite way, allow the blood in that cavity to pass into the lungs, but stop the blood in the lungs from returning to the heart; and two others at the entrance to the *arteria venosa*, which allow in the same way the blood from the lungs to flow towards the left cavity of the heart, but prevent it from returning; and three at the entrance to the *aorta*, which allow blood to leave the heart but stop it returning. And there is no need to look for any other cause for the number of these membranes other than that the aperture of the *arteria venosa*, being oval in shape on account of its location, can easily be closed with two of them, whereas the others, being round, can more easily be closed with three. Moreover, I would wish my readers to have pointed out to them that the *aorta* and the *vena arteriosa* are of a much harder and firmer texture than the *arteria venosa* and the *vena cava*, and that these latter two widen out before entering the heart to form two pouches, as it were, called the auricles of the heart, which are composed of similar substance to the heart itself. They will observe also that there is always more heat in the heart than in any other part of the body; and finally, that this heat is able to cause a drop of blood

49 entering its cavities to swell up at once and to dilate, in the

same way that all liquids do when they are allowed to fall drop by drop into a very hot vessel.

I have no need after this to say more to explain the movement of the heart, except that when its cavities are not full of blood, blood necessarily flows from the *vena cava* into the right cavity and from the *arteria venosa* into the left; for these two vessels are always full of blood, and their apertures, which open into the heart, cannot then be blocked; but, as soon as two drops of blood have entered the heart in this way, one into each cavity, these drops (which must very great, since the apertures by which they enter are very wide and the vessels from which they come are full of blood) rarify and dilate because of the heat they find there. In this way they cause the whole heart to swell, and they push shut the five little doors which are at the entrances of the two vessels from which they flowed, thus preventing any more blood coming down into the heart. Continuing to become more and more rarified, the drops of blood push open the six other little doors which are at the entrances of the two other vessels through which the blood leaves the heart, causing in this way all the branches of the *vena arteriosa* and the *aorta* to swell at more or less the same time as the heart.* Immediately afterwards the heart contracts, as do these arteries also, because the blood that has entered them has cooled, and their six little doors shut again; and the five doors of the *vena cava* and the *arteria venosa* open again and allow two new quantities of blood to pass through, which immedi- 50 ately cause the heart and the arteries to swell up as before. And because the blood that enters the heart in this way, passes through the two pouches which are called auricles, it follows from this that their movement is the opposite of the heart's, and that they contract when the heart swells. Finally, so that those who do not know the force of mathematical proof and are not used to distinguish true reasoning from *plausible* reasoning, should not venture to deny all this without examining it, I would like to point out to them that the movement I have just explained follows necessarily from the mere disposition of

41

organs that one can see with the naked eye in the heart, from the heat which one can feel there with one's fingers, and from the nature of blood which one can know from observation, in the same way as the movement of a clock follows from the force, position, and shape of its counterweights and wheels.*

But if one asks why the blood in the veins is not all used up by flowing continually in this way into the heart, and why the arteries are not too full because all the blood which passes through the heart goes into them, I need only repeat the answer already given by an English doctor, who must be praised for having broken the ice on this subject.* He was the first to show that there are many small passages at the extremities of the arteries through which the blood they receive from the heart enters the small branches of the veins, from which it immediately goes back to the heart, so that its course is nothing but a perpetual circulation. He proves this very well from the common experience of surgeons, who, having bound an arm moderately tightly above the point where they open a vein, make the blood flow out more abundantly than if they had not bound the arm. And the opposite would happen if they bound the arm below, between the hand and the vein being opened, or if they bound it very tightly above. For it is obvious that the moderately tight ligature, while being able to prevent the blood that is already in the veins from returning to the heart through the veins, cannot stop on that account fresh blood arriving from the arteries, because they are situated below the veins and their walls, being harder, are less easy to compress; and because the blood coming from the heart tends to flow through the arteries to the hand with greater force than it does when returning from the hand towards the heart through the veins. And because the blood comes out of the arm through the opening in one of the veins, there must necessarily be some passages below the ligature, that is to say, towards the extremities of the arm, through which it can come from the arteries. He also proves very well what he says about the circulation of the blood, first by certain small membranes

51

42

which are disposed at various points along the veins in such a way that they do not let blood pass from the centre of the body towards its extremities, but only permit it to return from the extremities towards the heart; second, by the experiment that shows that all the blood in the body can flow out of it in a very short space of time by a single artery when it is cut, even if it is tightly bound close to the heart, and cut between the heart and the ligature, so that there is no reason to imagine that the blood 52 that flows out comes from anywhere but the heart.

But there are many other things which are evidence of the fact that the true cause of this movement of the blood is as I have said it is. First, there is the difference to be observed between the blood which issues from the veins and that which issues from the arteries; this can only be due to the fact that, being rarefied, and, as it were, distilled in passing through the heart, it is thinner, more lively, and hotter straight after leaving it (that is to say, while in the arteries), than it is shortly before entering the heart (that is to say, while in the veins). And if one makes a careful observation, one will find this difference is only clearly perceptible close to the heart and not as perceptible in the parts most distant from it. Next, the hardness of the walls of which the *vena arteriosa* and the *aorta* are composed indicates clearly enough that blood beats against these more powerfully than against the veins. And why should the left cavity of the heart and the *aorta* be larger and wider than the right cavity and the *vena arteriosa*, if not because the blood of the *arteria venosa*, having been in the lungs only since it left the heart, is thinner and becomes more easily rarefied than the blood which flows directly from the *vena cava*? And what can physicians find out from taking the pulse if they did not know that, as the nature of blood changes, it can be rarefied by the heat of the heart to a greater or lesser degree and more or less quickly than before? And if we examine how this heat communicates itself to the other members of the body, must we not admit that this happens by means of the blood which is 53 reheated as it passes through the heart and spreads from there throughout the body? From which it follows that, if we remove blood from some part of the body, we remove heat by the same means as well, and even if the heart were as hot as a piece of glowing iron, it would not have sufficient heat to warm up the hands and feet as it does at present, unless it continually sent new blood to them. Then, too, we know from this that the true function of breathing is to bring enough fresh air into the lungs to cause the blood entering them from the right cavity into the heart, where it has been rarefied and, as it were, changed into vapour, to thicken up and convert itself once more into blood, before falling back into the left cavity; if it did not do this, it would not be fit to nourish the fire that is there. All this is confirmed by the fact that we see that animals not having lungs have also only one cavity in the heart, and that unborn children, who cannot use their lungs while in their mother's womb, have an aperture through which blood flows from the *vena cava* into the left cavity of the heart, and a duct by which it comes from the *vena arteriosa* to the *aorta*, without passing through the lung. And then, how could digestion occur in the stomach, if the heart did not send heat there through the arteries, together with some of the most fluid parts of the blood, which help to dissolve the food that we have ingested? And is it not easy to understand the action which converts the juice of this food into blood, if we consider that the blood is distilled perhaps more than one or two hundred times every day by passing repeatedly through the heart? And 54 what else is needed to explain nutrition and the production of the various humours* present in the body other than to say that the force with which the blood passes, as it rarefies, from the heart to the extremities of the arteries, causes some of its parts to come to rest in the parts of the members in which they then find themselves and there take the place of other parts which they expel; and that, according to the position, shape, or small size of the pores they encounter, some parts of the blood rather than others flow to certain places, in the same way that we see that sieves with different grades of mesh serve to separate different grains from each other? And finally, the most remarkable thing about all this is the generation of *animal spirits*,* which, like a very *subtle** wind, or rather like a very pure and living flame, rise continually in great abundance from the heart to the brain, pass from there through the nerves into the muscles, and impart movement to all our members. We do not need to suppose any other cause to impel the most agitated and the most penetrating parts of the blood (and hence the best suited to compose these spirits) to make their way to the brain rather than anywhere else, than that the arteries that carry them there are those which come most directly from the heart, and that, according to the rules of mechanics (which are the same as those of nature), when many things tend to move together towards the same place in which there is not room for them all (as in the case of the parts of the blood that leave the left cavity of the heart and flow towards the brain), the weaker or less agitated must of necessity be displaced by 55 the stronger, which by this means reach their destination on their own.

I had explained all these matters in considerable detail in the treatise which I had earlier intended to publish.* And I had then shown what structure the nerves and the muscles of the human body must have to enable the *animal spirits*, being inside that body, to have the power to move its members, as we observe in the case of severed heads, which we can see moving and biting the earth shortly after having been cut off, although they are no longer animate. I had also shown what changes must occur in the brain to cause states of waking, sleeping, and dreaming; how light, sounds, smells, tastes, heat, and all the other *qualities* of external objects can imprint various ideas on the brain through the intermediary of the senses; how hunger, thirst, and the other internal *passions* can also transmit ideas to the brain; what must be taken to be the *sensus communis** in which these are received, the *memory* which preserves them, and the *faculty of imagination*, which can change them in different ways, form them into new ideas and, by the same means, distribute animal spirits to the muscles and make the members of this body move, with respect both to the objects which present themselves to the senses and to the internal *passions*, in as many different ways as the parts of our bodies can move without being directed by our will. This will not appear at all strange to those who know how wide a range of different automata or moving machines the skill of man can make using only very few parts, in comparison to the great number of bones, muscles, nerves, arteries, veins, and all the other parts which are in the body of every animal. For they will consider this body as a machine which, having been made by the hand of God, is incomparably better ordered and has in itself more amazing movements than any that can be created by men.

At this point I had dwelt on this issue to show that if there were such machines having the organs and outward shape of a monkey or any other irrational animal, we would have no means of knowing that they were not of exactly the same nature as these animals, whereas, if any such machines resembled us in body and imitated our actions insofar as this was practically possible, we should still have two very certain means of recognizing that they were not, for all that, real human beings.* The first is that they would never be able to use words or other signs by composing them as we do to declare our thoughts to others. For we can well conceive of a machine made in such a way that it emits words, and even utters them about bodily actions which bring about some corresponding change in its organs (if, for example, we touch it on a given spot, it will ask what we want of it; or if we touch it somewhere else, it will cry out that we are hurting it, and so on); but it is not conceivable that it should put these words in different orders to correspond to the meaning of things said in its presence, as even the most dull-witted of men can do. And the second means is that, although such machines might do many things as well or even better than any of us, they would inevitably fail to do some others, by which we would discover that they did not act consciously, but only because their organs were disposed in a certain way. For, whereas reason is a universal instrument which can operate in all sorts of situations, their organs have to have a particular disposition for each particular action, from which it follows that it is practically impossible for there to be enough different organs in a machine to cause it to act in all of life's occurrences in the same way that our reason causes us to act.

Now we can also determine the difference between men and animals by these two means. For it is a very remarkable fact that there are no men so dull-witted and stupid, not even madmen, that they are incapable of stringing together different words, and composing them into utterances, through which they let their thoughts be known; and, conversely, there is no other animal, no matter how perfect and well endowed by birth it may be, that can do anything similar. Nor does this arise from lack of organs, for we can see that magpies and parrots can utter words as we do, and yet cannot speak like us, that is, by showing that they are thinking what they are saying; whereas men born deaf and dumb, who are deprived as much as, or more than, animals of the organs which in others serve 58 for speech, usually invent certain signs to make themselves understood by those who are their habitual companions and have the time to learn their language. This shows not only that animals have less reason than man, but that they have none at all.* For it is clear that we need very little reason in order to be able to speak; and given that as much inequality is found among animals of the same species as among men, and that some are easier to train than others, it is unbelievable that the most perfect monkey or parrot of their species should not be able to speak as well as the most stupid child, or at least a child with a disturbed brain, unless their soul were of a wholly different nature to ours. And speech must not be confused with the natural movements that are signs of passion and can be imitated by machines as well by as animals; neither must one imagine, as did certain ancient thinkers, that animals speak, although we do not understand their language. For if that were true, they would be able to make themselves understood by us as well as by other members of their species, since they have many organs that correspond to ours. It is also a very remarkable fact that although many animals show more skill in some of their actions than we correspondingly do, it is nonetheless clear than the same animals show none at all in many others, so that what they can do better than us does not prove that they have any mental powers, for it would follow from this that they 59 would have more intelligence than any of us, and would surpass us in everything. Rather, it shows that they have no mental powers whatsoever, and that it is nature which acts in them, according to the disposition of their organs; just as we see that a clock consisting only of ropes and springs can count the hours and measure time more accurately than we can in spite of all our *wisdom*.

Following this, I had described the rational soul, and shown that, unlike the other things of which I had spoken, it could not possibly be derived from the potentiality of matter, but that it must have been created expressly. And I had shown how it is not sufficient for it to be lodged in the human body like a pilot in his ship,* except perhaps to move its members, but that it needs to be more closely joined and united with the body in order to have, in addition, feelings* and appetites like the ones we have, and in this way compose a true man. I dwelt a little at this point on the subject of the soul, because it is of the greatest importance. For, after the error of those who deny the existence of God, which I believe I have adequately refuted above, there is none which causes weak minds to stray more readily from the narrow path of virtue than that of imagining that the souls of animals are of the same nature as our own, and that, as a consequence, we have nothing more to fear or to hope for after this present life, any more than flies and ants. But when we know how different flies and ants are, we can understand much better the arguments which prove that our soul is of a nature entirely independent of the body, and that, as a consequence, it is not subject to death as the body is. And given that we cannot see any other causes which may destroy the soul, we are naturally led to conclude that it is immortal.* 60

PART SIX

It is now three years since I completed the treatise that contained all the above. I was beginning to revise it so that I could place it in the hands of a printer, when I learned that persons to whom I defer, and whose authority holds hardly less sway over my actions than my own reason over my thoughts, had condemned a physical theory, published a little earlier by someone else,* to which I would not want to go so far as to say I subscribed, but only that I had seen nothing in it before their act of censure which I could imagine being prejudicial to religion or state, and which consequently would have prevented me from writing about it, if my reason had persuaded me to do so. This made me fear that there might be one of my own opinions in which I was equally mistaken, notwithstanding the great care I have always taken never to accept any new opinions for which I did not have very certain proof, and not to write about any which might work to the disadvantage of anyone. This was enough to make me change the decision I had taken to publish my theories. For even if the reasons for taking the decision earlier to publish were very strong, my natural inclination, which has always made me dislike the business* of writing books, led me to find a host of other reasons for excusing myself from doing so. And these reasons, both for and against, are such that not only do I have some interest in declaring them here, but the public may also have some interest in knowing what they are.

I have never laid great store by the products of my mind, and as long as I reaped no other benefits from the method that I use (apart from satisfying myself about some problems that belong to the speculative sciences, or trying to direct my life by the precepts that it inculcated in me), I have not felt obliged to write anything about it. For as far as mode of life is concerned, everyone is so sure that they know best that one could find as many reformers as there are people,* if it were permitted to any other than those whom God has established as sovereigns over their peoples, or those to whom He has given sufficient grace and zeal to be prophets, to set about changing anything. And although I was very pleased with my speculations, I believed that others had their own which perhaps pleased them even more. But having no sooner acquired some general notions about physics, and begun to test them out on various particular problems, I noticed where they may lead and how much they differ from the principles that have been employed up to now, and I believed that I could not keep them hidden without sinning greatly against the law that obliges us to procure, as far as it is in our power, the general good of all mankind. For these notions have made me see that it is possible to attain knowledge which is very useful in life, and that unlike the speculative philosophy that is taught in the schools, it can be turned 62 into a practice by which, knowing the power and action of fire, water, air, stars, the heavens, and all the other bodies that are around us as distinctly as we know the different trades of our craftsmen, we could put them to all the uses for which they are suited and thus make ourselves as it were the masters and possessors of nature.* This is not only desirable for the discovery of a host of inventions which will lead us effortlessly to enjoy the fruits of the earth and all the commodities that can be found in it, but principally also for the preservation of health, which is without doubt the highest good and the foundation of all the other goods of this life. For even the mind depends so much on the temperament* and disposition of the organs of the body that, if it is possible to find some way of making men in most cases wiser and more skilful than they have been hitherto, I believe that it is in medicine that it must be sought. It is true that medicine as presently practised contains little of such notable benefit; but without wishing to disparage it, I am certain that there is no one, even among those whose profession it is, who will not admit that what is known about it is almost nothing compared to what remains to be known, and that it would be possible to be free of innumerable illnesses of both body and mind, and perhaps even the decline of old age, if we knew enough about their causes and the 63 remedies with which nature has provided us.* So, intending to devote my whole life to the pursuit of such an indispensable branch of knowledge, and having found a path which, I think, will inevitably lead me to it, unless prevented from doing so by the brevity of life or the lack of *empirical information*, I judged that there was no better remedy against these two obstacles than to communicate faithfully to the public what little I had discovered, and to urge good minds to try to go further by contributing, each according to his inclinations and power, to the observations and experiments* that need to be undertaken, and by communicating in turn to the public everything that they learn. Thus, as the last would start from where their predecessors had left off, thereby combining the lives and labours of many, we might together make much greater progress than any one man could make on his own.

I noted, moreover, in respect of observations and experi-ments, that the further we progress in knowledge the more necessary they become. For, at the beginning, rather than to seek out rarer and more contrived experiments, it is better to undertake only those which communicate themselves directly to our senses, of which we cannot remain ignorant, provided that we reflect a little on them. The reason for this is that rarer experiments often mislead us, at a time when we do not still know the causes of more common ones, and the circumstances on which they depend are nearly always so *specific** and minute that it is difficult to take good note of them. But the order to which I have adhered in this regard is the following. First, I 64 have tried to find in general the principles or first causes of everything that exists or can exist the world, without consider-ing to this end anything other than God alone, who has created it, and deriving these principles only from certain seeds of truths which are naturally in our souls. After that, I came to examine what are the first and most common effects which one can deduce from these causes; and it seems to me that I have in this way discovered the heavens, heavenly bodies, and an earth; and, on the earth, water, air, fire, minerals, and several other such things which are the most common and the simplest of all, and hence the easiest to know. Then, when I wanted to proceed to more particular things, so many different ones presented themselves to me that I did not believe it possible for the human mind to distinguish the *Forms* or *Species** of bodies that are on the earth from a host of others which might be there, if it had been the will of God to put them there. Consequently, I did not think there was any other way to make them useful to us, than by progressing from effects to causes and by engaging in many individual observations. Following which, I cast my mind over all the objects that had ever presented themselves to my senses, and I venture to declare that I have not noticed anything which I could not explain quite easily by the principles I had found. But I must also acknowledge that the power of nature is so ample and vast, and these principles so simple and general, that I am able to observe hardly any particular effect without knowing from the beginning that it can be deduced from the principles in many different ways, and that my greatest difficulty is normally to find in which of these ways the effect depends on them. For I know of no other means of achieving this than by seeking further experiments and observations, whose results will vary according to the way the effect depends on my principles. For the rest, I have now reached the point where I think I can see quite clearly from which angle to approach most of the experiments and observations which can serve this end. But I can see also that they are of such a kind and in so great a number, that neither my industry nor my income (even if it were a thousand times greater than it is) could suffice for all of them. And so I will progress to a greater or lesser degree in knowledge of nature, according to the means that I have from now on to undertake more or less of them. I undertook to myself to make this known in the treatise I had written, and to show so clearly

65

53

the use the public may derive from it, that I would oblige all those who desire the good of mankind in general (that is to say, all those who are truly virtuous and do not just pretend to be, or just have that reputation) both to communicate to me the experiments and observations in which they have engaged and to help me in determining those which still need to be done.

Since that time I have, however, had other reasons to make me change my mind and decide that I had indeed to go on recording everything that I thought of some importance as I discovered the truth about it, and to bring the same care to this 66 task as if I intended to publish my results; as much in order to have more opportunity to examine them (as, without doubt, we always take greater care over what we think will be seen by many people than over what we do only for ourselves; and things which have seemed true to me when I began to think them out, have often seemed false when I have tried to set them down on paper), as to lose no opportunity to benefit the public, if I can, so that, if my writings are of any value whatsoever, those who will come into possession of them after my death will be able to make the most appropriate use of them. But I decided that I must never agree to them being published during my lifetime, to avoid being given occasion to waste the time I intend to use in acquiring knowledge, either on the opposition or the controversy to which they might be subject, or as a result of whatever reputation they might bring me. For although every man is indeed bound to procure the good of others insofar as it is within his power, and we are, in the true meaning of the word, worthless if we are of no use to anyone else, yet it is also true that our efforts have to reach out beyond the present time, and that it is acceptable to omit doing things which might bring some benefit to our contemporaries, when this is done in order to bring greater benefit to our grandchildren. I would also like it to be known that the little I have learnt up to now is almost nothing in comparison with what I do not know, and what I have not yet given up the hope of 67 coming to know; for those who gradually discover truth in the

54

sciences are more or less like people who, as they become wealthy, have less difficulty in making great acquisitions than they had earlier in making much smaller ones, when poorer. Or they can also be compared to military commanders, whose forces usually grow in proportion to their victories, and who need more skill to maintain their position after defeat in battle than they need to take towns and provinces after a victory. For to try to overcome all the problems and errors that prevent us attaining knowledge of the truth is indeed to engage in battle. And when we embrace some false opinion on a quite general and important matter, it is equivalent to losing one; much more skill is needed thereafter to regain the position we were in before, than in making great strides forward when we are already in possession of principles which are certain. For my part, if I have so far discovered a number of truths in the sciences (and I hope that the contents of this volume will cause people to think that I have indeed found a few), I can say that they merely result from and depend on my having overcome five or six principal difficulties, which I look on as so many battles in which I had good fortune to be on the winning side. I even dare speculate that I need only to win two or three others similar to these to fulfil my aims completely; and that I am not so advanced in age that I may not still have, in the ordinary course of nature, enough leisure to achieve this. But the 68 greater the hope I have of being able to spend the time that remains to me usefully, the more I see myself obliged to manage it carefully; and I would without doubt have many opportunities of wasting it, if I were to publish the foundations of my physics. For although they are nearly all so *incontrovertible* that one would only have to be apprised of them to believe them, and although there is not one among them which I do not think that I could prove, yet, since it is impossible that every one of them will be in agreement with all the different opinions of others, I foresee that I would be often distracted from my work by the hostile reactions to which they would give rise.

55

One might say that this opposition would be useful, as much to make my errors known to me as to allow others, if I had got something right, to understand it better; and since many can see more than one man can see by himself, it would allow them to help me with their discoveries as they began to use my own. But although I acknowledge that I am extremely prone to error, and that I almost never trust the first thoughts that come to me, nevertheless, the experience I have of the objections that can be made to my work prevents me from expecting any benefit from them. I have already often encountered the judgements, not only of those whom I have held to be my friends and some I thought indifferent to me, but also of certain others who, through malice and envy, would strive to expose what my friends did not see because of their affection for me. But it has rarely happened that objections have been made which I had not at all foreseen, except those which were not in any way pertinent to my work. Thus, I have almost never come across a critic of my opinions who did not seem either less exacting or less fair than myself. Nor have I ever found any previously unknown truth by means of the disputations that are practised in the schools;* for as long as the participants are trying to win, they are more concerned to make *plausibility* count than to weigh the two sides of the argument; and those who have long been good advocates do not necessarily go on to make better judges.

As for the benefit that others would receive from my thoughts being communicated to them, it might not be very great, seeing that I have not yet taken them so far that there is not much that needs to be added to them before putting them into practice. And I believe that I can say without vanity that if there is anyone capable of undertaking this, it must be myself rather than someone else; not that there may not be incomparably better minds than mine in the world, but because we cannot so well grasp something and make it our own when we learn it from someone else as when we discover it ourselves. This is so true in this case that, although I have often explained

69

some of my opinions to people endowed with very fine minds, and who, as I was telling them about them, seemed to understand them very clearly, yet when they repeated them back to me, I noticed that they had nearly always changed them in such a way that I could no longer acknowledge them as my own. I should like here to take this opportunity of asking 70 future generations never to believe that I am the source of the opinions people may tell them are mine, unless I have myself published them. I am in no way surprised by the extraordinary things which are attributed to all the ancient philosophers whose writings have not come down to us, nor do I conclude from this that their thoughts were very irrational (given that they were the best minds of their age), but only that they have been inaccurately reported to us. We see, too, that it has almost never happened that any of their disciples have surpassed them; and I am sure that the most passionate present-day followers of Aristotle would count themselves fortunate if they had as much knowledge of nature as he had, even on the condition that they would never have more. They are like ivy, which tends never to grow higher than the trees that support it, and often even grows back down once it has reached their tops. For it seems to me that modern Aristotelians also come back down, that is, make themselves in a certain way less knowledgeable than if they had abstained from study. Not content with knowing all that is intelligibly explained in their author, they wish, in addition, to find in his writings the solution to many problems about which he says nothing and to which he perhaps never gave any thought. However, their manner of philosophizing is very convenient to those who only have mediocre minds; for the obscurity of the distinctions and the principles which they use makes it possible for them to speak about the whole range of knowledge as boldly as if they really knew it all, and to maintain everything that they say against the subtlest 71 and shrewdest thinkers, without there being a means of causing them to change their minds. In this they seem to be like blind men who, in order to fight on equal terms against those who can see, lure them into the depths of some very dark cellar. I may say that it is in the interest of these people that I abstain from publishing the principles of philosophy that I use; for as they are very simple and very certain, I would be doing the same in publishing them as opening some windows, and letting the light of day into the cellar into which they have gone down to fight. But even the best minds have no reason to wish to know my principles; for if they want to be able to speak about everything and acquire the reputation of being learned, they will achieve this more easily by contenting themselves with *plausibility*, which can without great difficulty be found in all kinds of matters, than in seeking the truth, which is revealed only gradually in a few, and which requires, in any discussion of the others, that one frankly acknowledge one's ignorance. If they prefer the knowledge of a few truths to the vanity of appearing to know everything (and the former is, without doubt, preferable), and if they wish to pursue a project similar to mine, they do not in that case need me to say anything more to them than what I have already said in this discourse. For if they are capable of going beyond what I have done, they will be *a fortiori* capable of finding out for themselves everything I think I have discovered. And as I have never examined anything except in an orderly way, what

72 remains for me to discover is in itself certainly more difficult and more hidden than what I have been able to discover up to now, and they would have much less pleasure in learning it from me than for themselves.* Besides, the habit they will acquire of investigating easy things first and then progressing by degrees to other, more difficult matters will be of more use to them than all my instruction could be. And for my part, I am convinced that if I had been taught from my earliest years all the truths which I have since sought to prove, and had found no difficulty in learning them, I might perhaps never have known any others; or at least I would never have acquired the habit and facility which I think I have of always finding new ones, as I proceed to apply myself to search for them. In a

word, if there were in the world any one task which could not be better accomplished by anyone other than the person who began it, it is the one on which I am working.

Admittedly, as regards the experiments and observations that may be of use to this task, one man alone could not possibly do them all; but equally, he could not usefully employ other hands than his own, except those of artisans or such persons as he could pay, in whom the hope of gain (a very effective spur) would make them do exactly what he told them to do. For as for volunteers, who might offer to help him out of curiosity or a desire to learn, apart from usually promising more than they end up giving, and having fine proposals, none of which comes to fruition, they would inevitably wish to be 73 rewarded by having certain problems explained to them, or at least by compliments and vapid conversations which could not cost him so little time that he would not lose out by their involvement. And as for the experiments and observations that others have already made, even if they were willing to communicate them to him (something which those who call them secrets would never do*), they involve, for the most part, so many dependent circumstances and so many superfluous ingredients that it would be very difficult for him to determine the truth in them. Besides, he would find nearly all of them so badly explained or even so false, because those who undertook them had tried to make them appear to conform to their own principles, that even if there were some of which he could make use, they could not be worth the time he would have to spend selecting them. So if there were someone in the world who was known for sure to be capable of making discoveries of the greatest importance and public benefit, and that for this reason other men tried in every way possible to help him to achieve his ends, I do not see how they could do anything else for him, except to provide him with financial support for the experiments and observations he would need to make, and, for the rest, prevent his time being wasted by importunate visits from other people. But while not being so presumptuous as to be willing to promise remarkable results, nor entertaining thoughts so vain as to imagine that the public ought to take a great interest in my projects, I do not also have so base a soul as

74 to wish to accept from anyone whatsoever a favour which I might be deemed not to have deserved.

All these considerations taken together were the reason why, three years ago,* I refused to publish the treatise that I had in my hands, and why I had decided not to make public any other work in my lifetime which was so general, or from which one could derive the foundations of my physics. But two other reasons have since made me include here some individual essays,* and give the public some account of my actions and plans. The first is that if I failed to do so, many who know about my earlier intention to publish certain writings might imagine that the reasons why I have abstained from so doing were more to my discredit than they are. For although I am not excessively fond of glory, and even, if I dare say so, hate it, in that I judge it to be contrary to the tranquillity that I value above everything else, it is also the case that I have never tried to hide my actions as though they were crimes, nor have I taken great precautions to remain unknown; not only because I would have thought that I would be doing myself an injustice, but also because doing this would have given me a certain sort of uneasiness which would also have been opposed to the perfect peace of mind I am seeking. And because, although always having been indifferent to being well known or not known at all, I have been unable to avoid acquiring some sort of reputation, I have come to think that I must do my best to avoid

75 having a bad one. The other reason that has made me write is that of seeing every day the project that I have, to acquire knowledge, suffering more and more delay; because of the vast number of experiments and observations I need to make, and which it is impossible for me to undertake without the help of others. Although I do not flatter myself with any expectation that the public should share my interests, I do not, on the other hand, want to fall so far below my own standards that I give

those who come after me cause to reproach me one day for not having left them many things in better order than I have done, if I had neglected to make them see how they could contribute to my projects.

I believed it to be easy for me to choose certain matters which, without having been the subject of many controversies, nor compelling me to declare openly more of my principles than I wished, would still reveal quite clearly what I am capable, or not capable, of in the sciences. I cannot tell whether I have succeeded in this, and I do not want to prejudice anyone's judgement by speaking myself about my writings. But I shall be very glad for them to be critically examined, and so that one might feel all the more free to do so, I beg all those who may have any objections to take the trouble of sending them to my publisher, through whom, on being informed about them, I shall try to deliver my reply at the same time. By this means readers, seeing together the objections and the replies, will be able more easily to judge where the truth lies. I do not undertake ever to make long replies, but only to admit my mistakes frankly, if I perceive them, or, if I cannot see where they lie, to 76 say simply what I deem to be necessary in defence of what I have written, without proceeding to the explanation of any new matter, so as not to get dragged along interminably from one topic to the next.

If some of the things I speak about in the beginning of the *Dioptrics* and the *Meteorology* shock readers at first sight, because I call them '*suppositions*' and do not seem to want to prove them,* I ask them to have the patience to read the whole of the treatise attentively, and I hope that they will be satisfied by it. For it seems to me that my arguments follow each other in such a way that, if the last are proven by the first, which are their causes, the first are reciprocally proved by the last, which are their effects.* And one must not imagine that I am committing here the fallacy that logicians call a 'circle';* for as *empirical evidence** clearly confirms most of these effects, the causes from which I deduce them do not so much serve to prove them as to explain them; conversely, it is the causes that are proved by the effects. And I have called them 'suppositions' only to make it known that, while I think I can deduce them from the primary truths that I have explained above, I have expressly decided not to do this, in order to prevent certain thinkers from seizing the opportunity of building some new outlandish philosophy on what they believe to be my principles, for which I should be 77 blamed; thinkers who believe that as soon as one has said only two or three words to them on a given matter, they can know in one day what it would take someone else twenty years to think out; and the more penetrating and lively these thinkers are, the more they are liable to err and the less capable they are of the truth. As for the opinions that are wholly mine, I offer no apology for their being new;* for if the arguments supporting them are carefully considered, I am certain that one will find them so simple and so consistent with common sense, that they will seem less extraordinary and strange than any other opinions which one might entertain on the same subjects. I do not boast of being the first discoverer of any of them, but I do claim that I have accepted them, not because they have, or have not, been expressed by others, but only because reason persuaded me of their truth.

And if craftsmen are unable straight away to construct the invention explained in the *Dioptrics*, I do not believe that it can be said on that account to be bad. In view of the fact that it needs skill and practice to make and adjust the machines I have described, without missing out any detail, I would be no less surprised if they succeeded at the first attempt, than if someone could learn to play the lute expertly in a single day simply because he had been given a good fingering chart. And if I write in French, which is the language of my country, rather than Latin, which is that of my teachers, it is because I hope that those who use only their unalloyed natural reason will be better judges of my opinions than those who swear only by the books of the ancients.* And as for those who combine 78 good sense with application, whom alone I wish to have as my judges, I am sure they will not be so partial to Latin that they will refuse to grasp my arguments because I express them in the vulgar tongue.

For the rest, I do not wish to speak here in detail of the future progress I hope to make in the sciences, or commit myself to any promises to the public which I am not sure of being able to fulfil. I will simply say that I have decided to devote the rest of my life to nothing other than trying to acquire some knowledge of nature which may be such that we may derive some rules in medicine which are more reliable than those we have had up to now; and my inclination deters me so strongly from all other sorts of project, especially those which can be only useful to some by harming others,* that if some situation arose which forced me to work on them, I do not believe that I would be capable of succeeding. On this I here am making a declaration that I know will not make me worthy of esteem in the world, but then I have no desire to gain it. And I shall always consider myself more obliged to those through whose favour I may freely enjoy my time without hindrance, than to those who might offer me the offices in the world which are held in the highest esteem.

EXPLANATORY NOTES

3 *too long to be read all at once*: the *Discourse* is of course exceptionally short: Descartes is both commenting on the prolixity of his philosophical colleagues, and revealing his own dislike of reading long books: see AT 1. 221, 251; 3. 185 (letters to Mersenne, Oct. or Nov. 1631, 10 May 1632, 30 Sept. 1640); 5. 176–7 (a letter possibly to Huygens, 1642); 10. 214 (*Cogitationes privatae*: 'plerique libri, paucis lineis lectis figuris inspectis, toti innotescunt; reliqua chartae implendae adiecta sunt'), quoted above in translation, Introduction, p. xxiv.

5 *Good sense*: the Latin translation has *bona mens*; this is a collocation used by Seneca (*Epistulae morales*, 41. 1, 50. 17; *De vita beata*, 12. 1), but not in this sense. In Descartes's *Regulae*, 8, *bona mens* is glossed as 'universal wisdom' (*universalis sapientia*: AT 10. 360); what is designated here is the faculty of judgement which will allow us, if properly employed, to reach wisdom. Cf. letter to Mersenne, 16 Oct. 1639, AT 2. 597–8: 'all men having the same natural light [*lumière naturelle*, on which see below, note to p. 24, 'an inner light'], would seem to entail that all have the same notions . . . but . . . hardly anyone makes good use of this light.' Cf. Montaigne, *Essais*, ed. Pierre Villey (Paris 1965), 2. 17, 657: 'it is usually said that the most equitable distribution that nature has made to us of her gifts is that of the faculty of judgement'; also Romans 14: 5 (see also below, AT 6. 61, and note to p. 50, 'as many reformers'): 'let everyone abound in his own sense.' There are proverbs which make the same point: e.g. 'there are as many opinions as there are men' (*quot homines tot sententiae*). The concept of 'good sense' is discussed in the interview with Burman, AT 5. 175. Its possession by all men does not, however, exclude there being different degrees of aptitude for abstract thought (see below, AT 6. 58), or different degrees of success in using it correctly.

For it is not enough . . . correctly: Descartes has to make this point, because he will later argue that the consensus of the wise (the acknowledged experts in a given field)—(what is known in Latin at this time as *probabilitas*)—is not a sufficient argument to establish the truth of a proposition; the misapplication of good sense has led, in his contention, to the acceptance of many errors and the failure to discover many truths.

the right road . . . stray off it: the image, of the road and travelling, which recurs in the *Discourse*, is probably borrowed from Seneca, *De vita beata*, 1. 1, a text which he recommends to the Princess Elizabeth (AT 4. 253). This reminds us that Descartes had had an excellent humanist education, and that in spite of his declared hostility to reading, he had imbibed much of what he read.

make up an accomplished mind: the reference to reason ('mind'), imagination, and memory seems to be in accordance with traditional psychology, which assigned these faculties to three ventricles of the brain; but as will emerge later in the *Discourse*, reason, imagination, and memory are all immaterial, and do not have given locations, but only a place for interaction with the body (the pineal gland). See E. Ruth Harvey, *The Inward Wits* (London, 1975).

accidents . . . species: Descartes is here using scholastic vocabulary, and italicizes the technical words he is borrowing; but he cannot be said to reproduce scholastic doctrine, according to which reason, which defines man as a species of animal, must be equally present in all men; it is the degree to which the material part of man occludes its operation which explains difference of mental ability. Descartes cannot believe this, as he does not accept that there is any interaction between matter qua *res extensa* and mental activity qua *res cogitans*. There is a slight hint of mockery in the way he introduces the terms, hinting that they are empty verbiage. He makes use of this vocabulary at various points of the *Discourse*; subsequent italicization is my own (unless otherwise stated). On his use of these terms, see also Introduction, pp. l–li, lxvi.

6 *fashioned a method*: method is defined in *Regulae* 4 (AT 10. 371) as having four characteristics: certainty in the distinction between truth and error, ease of application, fruitfulness, and wisdom or the production of true knowledge.

vain and futile: i.e. philosophizing is the only non-futile human activity. The products to which Descartes refers include the treatises *Le Monde* (*The Universe*) and *L'Homme* (*Man*).

purely human occupations: Descartes consistently separates philosophy from theology or any grace-inspired speculations, and criticizes those who mix them together: e.g. Lord Herbert of Cherbury, whose *De veritate* (1624) is discussed in a letter to Mersenne of 29 Aug. 1639 (AT 2. 570). See also Introduction, pp. xii–xiii, on the possible hidden religious motive underlying his own practice of philosophy.

the reactions . . . to this picture: an allusion to the practice of the Greek painter Apelles, who hid behind his canvases to hear what the public would say about them (hence the saying *Apelles latens post tabulam*); the Latin translation of the *Discourse* at this point makes the allusion explicit by citing the saying; Descartes refers to the practice in a letter to Mersenne dated 8 Oct. 1629 (AT 1. 23).

tried to conduct mine: cf. Montaigne, *Essais*, ed. Pierre Villey (Paris, 1965) 3. 2, pp. 804–6: 'others educate man; I am giving an account . . . of one particularly badly educated one . . . I'm not teaching, I'm telling a story' ('les autres forment l'homme; je le recite . . . et en represente un particulier bien mal formé . . . je n'enseigne poinct, je raconte').

7 *classical studies*: *lettres*; Descartes was educated at the Jesuit Collège de la Flèche, where he received the standard humanistic education, which extended beyond what we would understand by 'letters'; in the next few pages he sets out the curriculum he followed. See Introduction, pp. ix–x.

occult and recondite: a reference to the 'low sciences' of astrology, chiromancy, natural magic, and alchemy. Chiromancy had been condemned and banned in a papal bull of 1586.

8 *oratory ... delicacy and charm*: oratory is the fruit of classical rhetoric; the poetry referred to comes from the pens of classical authors such as Virgil, Horace, Statius, Ovid, and Claudian.

books on morals ... virtue: the two most cited ancient moralists were Seneca and Plutarch; but these and other pagan writers will be attacked in the next paragraph for their un-Christian attitudes.

riches and honours: Descartes is here referring to a cynical adage about the faculties of medicine and law: 'Galen brings riches and Justinian honour; from other disciplines you gather chaff, from these two grain' ('dat Galenus opes et sanctio Justiniana | ex aliis paleas, ex istis collige grana'). He seems to suggest that a complete education will include the higher faculties of law and medicine, which are only taught in universities, not in Jesuit colleges; he went on to study the law himself at the University of Poitiers, but does not refer to this part of his education here. See Introduction, pp. ix–x.

9 *knights of old*: 'les paladins de nos romans'; Descartes is referring to the medieval tales of heroic chivalry which were still popular in his day.

thickest of dialects: *bas breton*: the dialect of lower Brittany was particularly decried in Descartes's day for its barbarity; in his unpublished *Pursuit of Truth* (*Recherche de la vérité*), Descartes cites Swiss French with Breton as particularly rustic dialects. Montaigne makes the same point about the natural powers of argumentation found among the uninstructed (*Essais*, 3.8, p. 925).

incontrovertibility: *evidence*: on this term, see the Introduction, p. l.

mechanical arts: at La Flèche geography, hydrography, military arts, and mechanics were taught, in addition to the subjects prescribed in the Jesuit *Ratio studiorum*, on which see Introduction, pp. ix–x, and Stephen Gaukroger, *Descartes: An Intellectual Biography* (Oxford, 1992), 38–67.

lack of human feeling ... parricide: see above, note to p. 8 'books on morals ...'. This is the traditional Christian line of attack on Stoic philosophy; Descartes, like many of his contemporaries, approves of other versions of Stoic philosophy, such as the *Handbook* of Epictetus: see Introduction, p. lii.

10 *... more than merely human*: Descartes is referring to divine grace; in Catholic theology, this confers on those who receive it (for example,

ordained priests) powers in excess of merely human mental capacities, and qualifies them to discuss doctrine and interpret Holy Writ. On his reticence about his own divine calling, and his keenness to avoid any suggestion that he was laying claim to special powers, see note to p. 6, 'purely human occupations' above, and Introduction, pp. xii–xiii.

plausible: *vraisemblable*. Descartes consistently tries to rid himself of the middle category of merely plausible propositions, those described by the Latin terms *probabiles* (i.e. being approved of by the wisest in a given area, or being derived from textual authority) and *verisimiles* (i.e. that which can plausibly be derived from the evidence of the senses). These were accepted in such disciplines as law and medicine: see Ian Maclean, *Logic, Signs and Nature in the Renaissance: The Case of Learned Medicine* (Cambridge, 2001), 128–37; see also below, note to p. 16, 'the majority view'.

the habit of Cynics: a reference to the ancient philosophical sect whose most famous member was Diogenes of Sinope (*c.*400–*c.*325 BC).

the low sciences: there is a subsequent reference to these hermetic and occult arts and their habit of preserving 'secrets': see below, p. 59. Descartes is very keen to have his own practice of science, and his own promises of providing enlightenment, clearly distinguished from them.

11 *had persuaded me of*: Descartes attributes here to his experience what he also might have learned from his reading of Montaigne's *Essais* (especially 1. 23, 1. 31, and 2. 12).

12 *emotional turmoil*: *passions*: Descartes was to write a treatise entitled *The Passions of the Soul* in the 1640s, in which the term reflects neo-Stoic usage, and designates those perturbations of the mind which are occasioned by consideration of future, present, or past good or evil.

a small room . . . at leisure: the Thirty Years War, to which Descartes is referring here, lasted from 1618 to 1648; the coronation in question was that of the Holy Roman Emperor Ferdinand II at Frankfurt am Main, which took place between 20 July and 9 September 1619. The army mentioned here is that of the Catholic Elector Maximilian, duke of Bavaria. The quarters are thought to have been either in a village near Ulmor or near Neuburg. The single day of solitary reflection and enlightenment in the stove-heated room referred to here is dated by Descartes's early biographer Adrien Baillet to 10 November 1619.

designs . . . on an empty plain: Descartes may have in mind the town of Richelieu, designed *de novo* by the architect Lemercier to a strict geometrical pattern on a plain, and built in the 1630s for the chief minister of France, Cardinal Armand du Plessis de Richelieu; this was situated less than 20 km from his family's possessions in Poitou.

13 *contrary to good morals*: Descartes is here apparently breaking his own rule about passing value judgements on the customs and morals of other

nations (see above, AT 6. 10). Among the practices he may have in mind are the exposure on hillsides of deformed children, the encouragement given to citizens to spy on one another, nudity in gymnastics for both sexes, and women shared as sexual partners by certain groups.

13 *by one man*: the single lawgiver of Sparta was reputed to be Lycurgus.

. . . guided by that alone: Descartes offers a model of human development in which the immaterial soul gradually frees itself from the material body, in which are located '[animal] appetites'. This has implications both for the relationship between will (the 'rational appetite') and desire, and the nature of the will itself, which are not fully worked out until the treatise on the *Passions of the Soul*. See below, note to p. 24, 'an inner light'.

14 *in schools for teaching it*: reference to the Aristotelian curriculum in the schools, on which see Introduction, pp. ix–x; Descartes does not wish to declare himself to be a revolutionary, but clearly intends to be one.

political judgement: prudence (*prudentia*, *phronesis*): the faculty traditionally associated with 'practical' philosophies (politics, ethics, and domestic management). The sentiments expressed here, and those which follow, are very close to those to be found in Montaigne, *Essais*, 1. 23 and 1. 31.

15 *more lofty designs*: on the privileges bestowed by divine grace, see notes to pp. 6, 'purely human occupations' and 9, 'lack of human feeling', above.

less capable . . . themselves: this seems to be in conflict with the notion of a generally equal distribution of good sense expressed at the beginning of the *Discourse*.

no opinion . . . some philosopher or other: reminiscence of Cicero, *De divinatione*, 2. 58. 119: 'in some way or other there is nothing so absurd that can be said that has not been said by one or other of the philosophers' ('sed nescio quo modo nihil tam absurde dici potest quod non dicatur ab aliquo philosophorum').

16 *the majority view*: la pluralité des voix (Latin: *multitudo suffragiorum*). It seems likely that Descartes has in mind here either the definition of 'probable' given in Aristotle's *Topics* (i. 1, 100b 22 f., as 'generally accepted . . . commending itself to all or to the majority of the wise', or its legal equivalent, known as 'common opinion' (*opinio communis*), on which see Ian Maclean, *Interpretation and Meaning in the Renaissance: The Case of Law* (Cambridge, 1992), 93. We may note again Descartes's aversion to accepting plausibility in any of its guises.

the art of Lull . . . anything new: the Catalan philosopher and theologian Raymond Llull (1232–?1315) set out to provide in his *Ars magna* a universal method of discovery. Isaac Beeckman discussed Llull with Descartes (AT 10. 156, 164–7), but it appears that Descartes never took the text seriously (AT 2. 629). It was commonly argued against syllogisms that they revealed nothing new.

17 *block of marble*: Descartes here wittily adapts an analogy from Aristotelian philosophy for his own purposes; in *Physics*, i. 7 (190b 7), *Metaphysics*, iii. 5 (1002a 21–2), and v. 7 (1017b 6–7), Aristotle uses the example of a statue of 'Hermes' (not Diana or Minerva) being in the stone from which it will be carved to show the distinction between potentiality and actuality; Descartes has no time for this metaphysical distinction.

slave to certain rules and symbols . . . cultivates it: on Descartes's revision of the mathematical notation of his day, see Introduction, pp. lxii–lxiii. He is likely to have encountered modern versions of mathematics both in La Flèche, where the work of the Jesuit defender of mathematics Christophorus Clavius was known, and in Paris in the Mersenne circle, members of which were aware of the work of recent French scholars such as François Viète.

The first . . . no occasion to doubt it: on these precepts, see Introduction, pp. xlix–li.

positing: *supposant*: this usage is close to that of natural philosophers of Descartes's generation, for whom *suppositiones* are 'those things which must be accepted from the outset before a science can be constructed— definitions, statements of existence and undemonstrated (though not unjustified) principles generally' (Peter Dear, 'Jesuit Mathematical Science and the Reconstitution of Experience in the Early Seventeenth Century', *Studies in the History and Philosophy of Science*, 18 (1987), 148). Reasoning *ex suppositione* assumes that the empirical fact, the process, to be explained—acorns developing into oak-trees, for example—was taken or supposed to have actually occurred without impediment (William Wallace, *Prelude to Galileo: Essays on Medieval and Sixteenth-Century Sources of Galileo's Thought* (Dordrecht, 1981), 129–59). The question of supposition will come up again (see AT 6. 42, 44–5, 76); here Descartes merely attributes supposition to the order in which a problem is addressed.

a natural order of precedence: the order suggested here by Descartes does not specify which the 'most easily understood objects' are; in traditional Aristotelian terms, a distinction is made between that which is 'better known by its nature' and that which is 'better known to us' (*Prior Analytics*, 71b 9–12; ii. 23, 68b 15 ff. *Physics*, i. 1. 184a 16–21; *Metaphysics*, i. 2, 982a 25). The latter is known initially through the senses; the former is a universal which is derived from the accumulation of sensory particulars (*Prior Analytics*, ii. 27). The nature of knowledge received into the mind is such that universals are better known to it than the particulars of sensory experience. The alternative ancient view is the Platonic view of reminiscence (on which see *Meno*, 70A ff.), according to which there is no such thing as discovery, because if we do not know, we will not recognize what we have found, and if we know in fact, then we have no reason to enquire. What is in question here is both the method of discovery of universal terms in 'science' and the method of presentation of the results of such enquiry; Descartes presents his method as one of discovery, and does not concern himself here with the pedagogical implications of the order of presentation. His argument that metaphysics precedes physics relegates sensory knowledge from its primordial place: see Introduction, p. li.

17 *. . . left nothing out*: the three elements of the method—division, simplification, enumeration—are interdependent and imply each other (*Regulae*, 7, AT 10. 392); they also can have a relationship to induction (ibid., AT 10. 390), but only in cases where the cases cited show that no other case can be later conceived which would invalidate the conclusion (e.g. that the area of a circle is greater than all other figures having the same periphery). Each element of the enumeration for Descartes is confirmed by the intuition of its clearness, distinctness, and evidentness as a reliable building-block for further deductions; such a test is much more rigorous than the empirical version of induction set out, for example, by Francis Bacon in Book 2 of his *Novum organum*.

18 *. . . one cannot discover it*: this is Descartes's version of the *mos geometricus*, which is praised as a procedure by a number of ancient philosophers (among them Galen), and their Renaissance followers (Cardano).

under the name of mathematics: in Descartes's day, it was habitual to distinguish pure mathematics from mixed mathematics, which included astronomy, astrology, music, mechanics, and optics.

these proportions in general: a simple set of proportions are equality, being greater, and being less (a = b; a > b; a < b); *Regulae*, 14 (AT 10. 451) divides these relations into two categories, order and measure. Order requires nothing other than sequence (a, b); measure requires a third term (a unit which is the common measure).

to my imagination: whether proportions should be thought about with visual aids or only with the use of symbols is discussed in *Regulae*, 15–16, AT 10. 453–9. Below (AT 6. 37–9) Descartes states that imagination has no role to play in metaphysical speculation; he makes the contrast with mathematics very clear in a letter to Mersenne of 13 November 1639 (AT 2. 622): 'the part of the mind which is of most use in mathematics, namely the imagination, is more of a hindrance than a help in metaphysical speculations'; see also AT 5. 177.

19 *briefest possible symbols*: on the elegance of Cartesian notation (which was substantially achieved also a little earlier by Thomas Harriot, although there is no way of showing that Descartes was aware of this), see above, note to p. 17, 'slave to certain rules . . .' and *Introduction*, pp. lxii–lxiii.

months I spent investigating them: according to Étienne Gilson, *Discours de la méthode: texte et commentaire* (Paris, 1925), 222–3, the period in question must lie between December 1619 and February 1620.

other branches of knowledge: Descartes has in mind especially physics or natural philosophy (he describes himself as 'physico-mathematicus' even before 1619: see AT 10. 52).

21 *a provisional moral code*: it has been argued that Descartes claimed to have achieved considerable progress towards a definitive version of ethics, and that this is enshrined in the *Treatise on the Passions*, which appeared in 1649: see Anthony Levi, *French Moralists: The Theory of the Passions 1585 to 1649* (Oxford, 1964), 257–98; but in the preface to the *Principia* (AT 9. 14) the 'highest ethics' is said only to be possible after a complete grasp of all other branches of knowledge had been achieved.

customs of my country: on obedience to local custom, see note to p. 14, 'political judgement'.

. . . *rather than what they said*: Montaigne makes the same point aphoristically (*Essais*, 1. 26, 168): 'the true mirror of our discourse is the course of our lives' ('le vray miroir de nos discours est le cours de nos vies').

. . . *know that we believe it*: this distinction is made in more general terms by Aristotle (in knowing the object of our mind's thought, we know at the same time our mind: *De anima*, iii. 4–5); this gives rise to much speculation about the relationship of the mind to the knowledge of itself as an object of thought in the Renaissance (see Ian Maclean, 'Language in the Mind: Reflexive Thinking in the Late Renaissance', in *Philosophy in the Sixteenth and Seventeenth Centuries: Conversations With Aristotle*, ed. Constance Blackwell and Sachiko Kusukawa (Aldershot, 1999), 195–321). Descartes seems here to be dividing an act of the will (the judgement that something is good or bad) from the intellect's awareness of that judgement. Both the will and the intellect fall within the *cogitatio* or thinking which provides the immediate intuition of existence: see *Principia*, 1. 9, AT 8A. 7.

22 *most certain ones*: *constamment*: a word which evokes neo-Stoic virtue, on which see Introduction, pp. lii–liii.

23 *probability*: *probabilité*: on this term, see above, notes to pp. 5, 'For it is not . . .'; 10, 'more than merely human'; and 16, 'the majority view'.

. . . *as far as we are concerned*: on the parallel of this sentiment, and those which follow, with the philosophy of Epictetus, see Introduction, p. lii.

periods of meditation: Justus Lipsius' *Introduction to Stoic Philosophy* (*Manuductio ad stoicam philosophiam*, 3. 24) of 1604 ends with an exhortation to long meditation; Descartes would also have been familiar with St Ignatius Loyola's *Spiritual Exercises*, which also prescribe this form of mental activity. The *Meditations* of 1641 may well owe their title and division into six parts to the latter author's work.

24 *rival their gods in happiness*: a reference to ancient Stoic philosophers, and more especially to a text in Seneca (*Epistulae*, 73. 13: 'a god has no

advantage over a wise man in respect of happiness, even though he has such an advantage in respect of years' ('deus non vincit sapientem felicitate, etiam si vincit aetate').

24 *however favoured . . . they may be*: a reference to Cicero's *Paradoxa stoicorum*, 5 ('that the wise man [i.e. the Stoic sage] alone is free') and 6 ('that the wise man alone is rich').

an inner light: this is the natural light of reason discussed in Cicero's *Tusculan Disputations*, 3. 1. It was a phrase taken up by occult philosophers such as Oswald Croll at the beginning of the seventeenth century, and contrasted with the light of grace: 'two lights are known from which comes all perfect knowledge and besides which there is none. The light of grace gives birth to the true theologian, when accompanied by philosophy. The light of nature brings the philosopher into being, when accompanied by theology, which is the foundation of true wisdom.' Their critics point to the risks of disciplinary anarchy in such a doctrine: 'they make up some light of nature and grace or other,' writes Daniel Sennert, 'with which they disguise the figments of their brain that cannot be proved by either reason or experience. If it is permitted for any new dogma to be brought forth free of all experience and reason, and that credence should be given to it by simple reference to the light of nature and of grace, the result will be that truth will be what it seems to be to anyone. No-one can fail to see what confusion would come from this in every discipline.' See Maclean, *Logic, Signs and Nature*, 199–200. Descartes is not writing in the context of this debate, but is aware of the problem which arises when the 'light of nature' is invoked; his solution (sometimes called the 'rationalist' one) is to argue that the mind possesses (innate) fundamental truths independent of the senses from which it is possible to deduce the elementary truths of mathematics and natural philosophy.

25 *. . . to do our best*: this is very close to the Thomist doctrine expressed in *Summa Theologiae*, 1a 2ae 8, 1, according to which the will is a rational appetite which desires what is good, or what it perceives to be good (hence correct judgement equates to virtue, and vice to error; or as Descartes puts it in a letter to Mersenne dated 27 April 1637, 'anyone sinning sins out of ignorance'. The rational appetite is distinguished from the animal appetite (already invoked: see above, note to p. 13, 'guided by that alone').

the next nine years: i.e. from 1619 to 1628; for an account of the known travels of these years, see Gilson, *Discours*, 265–6, Stephen Gaukroger, *Descartes: An Intellectual Biography* (Oxford, 1995), 132–4, and Geneviève Rodis-Lewis, *Descartes: His Life and Thought*, trans. Jane Marie Todd (Ithaca and London, 1998), 49–72.

reach a decision: Descartes is here referring to a specific Pyrrhonist (sceptical) practice of countering any proposition with its opposite, and suspending judgement (the ways of arguing known as *phonoi skeptikoi*). It is described by Montaigne, in *Essais*, 2. 12, pp. 504–5. How seriously Descartes took this doctrine to be a threat to good philosophical practice is a matter of dispute. He employs doubt as a means of establishing where error lies, not as an excuse for suspension of judgement.

26 *many experiences*: *expériences* (Latin: *experimenta*): this word can denote the products of sensory perception, or experiments; it will be translated as 'observations and experiments' when it occurs in contexts in which its sense is not restricted to one or the other of these meanings. See Peter Dear, *Discipline and Experience: The Mathematical Way in the Scientific Revolution* (Chicago and London, 1995).

. . . *dealt with in this volume*: Descartes may be referring here particularly to the laws of sines which are discussed in the *Dioptrics* and the discussion of the rainbow in the *Meteorology*.

than read books: on Descartes's aversion to reading see above, note to p. 3, 'too long'.

excellent minds . . . succeeded: see Introduction, pp. xlix–l, for more modern names: Descartes may be referring here also to Aristotle (especially the *Posterior Analytics*) and Galen (the *Ars parva*).

27 *to retire here*: Descartes moved to Holland in 1629; the war to which he is referring is that between the United Provinces and Spain, which lasted from 1572 to 1648, with a truce from 1609 to 1621.

. . . *the most populous cities*: cf. Introduction, p. xi (letter to Balzac of 5 May 1631, AT 1. 203).

28 *our senses sometimes deceive us . . . imagine it to be*: doubting the evidence of the senses is of course a commonplace, much employed to reduce man's presumptuous confidence in the knowledge he possesses. Descartes links it here to the question of the illusory experiences of dreams.

. . . *accepted as valid proof*: Descartes omits here the argument of the 'malin génie', which appears in the first Meditation (AT 7. 22–3); there he conjures up a powerful and ingenious demon who devotes all his efforts to making him believe what was not true. It is possible that he thought that this was too radical and threatening for his non-professional readers.

I am thinking therefore I exist: the Latin version reads *cogito ergo sum*, which is normally translated as 'I think therefore I am'; but the glosses that Descartes places on this elsewhere (notably in the second parts of the *Principia* and the *Meditations*) make it clear both that it is a performative ('I am thinking') and that being is existing; he is not referring to being as essence: cf. *Principia*, 1. 7, AT 9B. 7: 'it is contradictory to suppose that what is thinking does not, at the very time when it is thinking, exist.' Two other points emerge from this passage: the first step towards the *cogito* is in fact the *dubio* ('I am doubting, therefore I am existing'); and the immediacy of this intuition is not consistent with the view expressed by other Renaissance figures who consider reflexive thinking, such as Cardano, who see a time interval elapsing between the thought and the realization that the thought is being thought (*De libris propriis*, ed. Ian Maclean (Milan, 2004), 328): 'we do not know and know that we are knowing in the same moment, but a little before or after' ('eodem momento non intellig[i]mus, et cognosc[i]mus nos intelligere, sed paulo ante vel post'). For a different critique of the human subject being simultaneously the object and subject of its own enquiry, see Anthony Kenny, *The Anatomy of the Soul: Historical Essays in the Philosophy of Mind* (Oxford, 1973).

28 *certain*: *assurée*; from now on, *évidence* is equated with certainty. The reply to the sceptics takes their rallying-cry *epecho* ('I doubt') and shows that it entails existence. Both Mersenne (as revealed by Descartes's letter to him of 25 May 1637: AT 1. 376), and Antoine Arnauld in his objections to the *Meditations* (AT 7. 197), point to the fact that a similar argument appears at various points in St Augustine's writings: *De libero arbitrio*, 2. 3. 7; *De civitate Dei*, 9. 26; also *De trinitate*, 10. 10. 14. Here the reply to the sceptical attack on the knowledge of the self, 'what if you are wrong?', reads 'if I am wrong, I am' (*si fallor, sum*). Descartes first claimed not to have used the argument in the same way as Augustine, and returned to the point in a later letter of December 1640 (AT 3. 261), where he links it with the supposed similarity Mersenne must have perceived between Descartes's (a posteriori) proof of God's existence and the (a priori) ontological proof of God by St Anselm, on which see note to p. 30, 'which was God', and Introduction, p. lvii.

principle . . . I was seeking: this first principle is not the same as a syllogistic premiss or conclusion, but some of Descartes's contemporaries tried to translate it into those terms, to his manifest annoyance: see Introduction, p. lv.

29 *the Soul*: *Ame*: the capitalization makes clear that Descartes wishes the word to be read in its highest (theological) context; a usage reinforced by the previous use of 'substance' and 'essence'. *Ce moi* ('This I'), which turns the first-person pronoun into a noun, is a neologism; but it would be mistaken to believe that, without it, a certain sort of objectified or transcendental self-reference was not possible. Cf. Montaigne's use of *âme* with the first-person pronoun in *Essais*, 3. 5, p. 876.

30 *. . . lacking something*: it is a Cartesian principle that truth consists in being, and falsity only in non-being: see the letter to Clerselier of 23 April 1649 (AT 5. 357): 'it is clear to me by the natural light [see above, note to p. 24, "an inner light"] that all deception depends on a defect; for a being in which there is no imperfection cannot tend to non-being, that

is, cannot have non-being, or non-goodness or non-truth as its end and purpose, for these three are the same' ('omnem fraudem a defectu pendere, mihi est lumine naturali manifestum; quia ens in quo nulla est imperfectio, non potest tendere in non ens, hoc est, pro fine et instituto suo habere non ens, sive non bonum, sive non verum; haec enim tria idem sunt').

. . . that something should proceed from nothing: Descartes refers here to a premiss of both atomistic and Aristotelian physics ('nihil ex nihilo fieri'), which was condemned by the bishop of Paris in 1277 because it was inconsistent with the Judaeo-Christian doctrine of creation; he employs it here, as in his reply to the third objections to the *Meditations* (AT 7. 40) makes explicit, to argue that 'there is no thing, nor any actual existing perfection of a thing, which can have nothing or a non-existence thing as the cause of its existence' ('nulla res, nec ulla rei perfectio actu existens, potest habere nihil, sive rem non existentem, pro causa suae existentiae').

30 *. . . which was God*: Descartes's proof of God is compared by his contemporaries to the (a priori) ontological proof of God's existence by St Anselm, to which Mersenne drew Descartes's attention (see AT 3. 261), in which God is defined as a being than which nothing greater can be conceived, and it is argued that such a being cannot exist in the understanding alone, but must exist in reality, which is greater than that which resides only in the understanding. It is also compared to the proof of God offered by Aquinas in *Summa Theologiae*, 1a 2,1 by Pierre Bourdin in the first objections to the *Meditations* (AT 7. 96–9). There is a very clear account of these complex and disputed arguments, and their relationship to Descartes's own argument and its claim to be novel, in Gilson, *Discours*, 324–39.

to have, of myself . . . participation . . . knew myself to lack: the italicized words are those which Descartes is using in a technical way ('I shall here freely employ, with your permission, some scholastic terminology'). In fact, he had begun earlier with substance and essence.

31 *manifestly a defect*: because the parts of a composite thing depend on the whole, and the whole on the parts, both are seen as lacking the perfection of independent existence.

or other intelligences: *intelligences*: immortal incorporeal beings in scholastic philosophy.

. . . without Him: the doctrine that God intervenes at every moment in his creation to ensure its continuing existence is known as occasionalism; the unique feature of Cartesian occasionalism is that it is not linked to substantial forms or essences; see Gilson, *Discours*, 341–2. This, and such attributes as infinite and eternal, were much discussed in Descartes's time in natural philosophy and medicine: see Maclean, *Logic Signs and Nature*, 89–90.

32 *proof that God . . . exists*: this argument, known as the 'ontological proof', was widely attacked by Descartes's contemporaries (see AT 7. 98, 115, 127, 149, 152, 320, 382–4 and above, note to p. 30, 'which was God').

unimaginable . . . unintelligible: on the use of imagination, see above, note to p. 18, 'to my imagination'.

. . . *previously been in the senses*: on the Aristotelian adage 'Nil in intellectu quod non fuerit prius in sensu', see Introduction, p. li. Descartes effectively reverses the adage.

we possess an assurance: une assurance morale: by 'moral assurance' is meant here a certainty sufficient for ordinary practical purposes: *Principes*, 4, AT 9. 323–4.

33 . . . *comes from Him*: this passage gave rise to the objection that the argument was circular: it was alleged that Descartes determines an idea to be clear and distinct because God exists, is the author of the idea, and is not a deceiving God; and determines that there is a God, that He is the creator, and that He is the source of all truth and nothing but truth, because there is a clear and distinct idea of Him: see Gassendi's comments in the fourth objections to the *Meditations*, AT 7. 214.

. . . *not wholly perfect*: an expanded version of this condensed passage of reasoning is found in *Meditations*, 4, AT 7. 55 ff.

34 . . . *without our being asleep*: on the relation of this passage, in which dreams are taken to be material, and Descartes's prophetic dream of 10 November 1619, see Introduction, pp. xii–xiii.

a chimera exists in the world: reminiscence of Aristotle, *De interpretatione*, i. 1, 16a 16 f.: 'tragelaphos [goat-deer], while it means something, has no truth or falsity in it, unless in addition you predicate being or non-being of it.'

must infallibly: Descartes felt uncomfortable about the strength of this claim, and approved of the change of 'infallibly' to 'rather' (*potius*) in the Latin translation of 1644.

35 *certain considerations . . . from publishing*: on Galileo's trial, and Descartes's correspondence with Mersenne, see Introduction, pp. xxviii–xl. Two parts of the treatise mentioned here (*Le Monde*; *L'Homme*) were published posthumously from (incomplete) manuscripts: see AT 11. 1–290.

36 *if God . . . in imaginary space*: this hypothesis at one remove allows Descartes to avoid citing condemned doctrines after the condemnation of Galileo: see Introduction, p. xxxviii. In considering this hypothetical universe, he avoids also taking a position over the finiteness or infiniteness of the universe, insisting only that it is for his purposes indefinite (*Principia*, 1. 26, AT 8A. 14–15), and citing later, in a letter to Chanut of 6 June 1647 (AT 5. 51), one Church authority (the fifteenth-century

bishop Nicholas of Cusa) on his side: 'I remember that Cardinal Nicholas of Cusa and many other doctors [of the Church] have supposed the universe to be infinite, without ever being reprimanded by the Church on this point.'

forms or qualities: on the setting aside of these terms, see Introduction, pp. l–li.

37 *on the subject of light*: on the content of the treatise on light, see Introduction, p. xxvii.

conferred no weight: *pesanteur*: in scholastic terms, the tendency of bodies to go downwards (see Aristotle, *On the Heavens*, 4).

38 *. . . by which He created it*: on this doctrine, see Aquinas, *Summa Theologiae*, 1a 104.1 ad 4.

casting doubt upon the miracle of creation: on the sensitivity of this point, see above, note to p. 30, 'that something should proceed from nothing', and Introduction, p. xxviii.

rational . . . vegetative or sensitive soul: on the Aristotelian theory of the tripartite soul see Harvey, *The Inward Wits*. All that is left after this subtraction is extension and movement.

41 *. . . same time as the heart*: this perpetuates the Galenic view, according to which the pulse corresponds to diastole and is the active phase, and systole is the passive phase of muscular relaxation in the heart; Harvey's view that systole is the active phase is now taken to be correct against Descartes.

42 *. . . counterweights and wheels*: the point of this passage—the reduction of the movement of the heart to a mechanical explanation (i.e. the subtraction of any reference to occult forces)—is forcefuly made by this analogy.

English doctor . . . on this subject: the marginalium here reads 'Hervaeus, *de motu cordis*'; the reference is of course to William Harvey's *On the Motion of the Heart and Blood in Animals* (1628), a text to which Mersenne drew Descartes's attention (see the letter to Mersenne of November or December 1633, AT 1. 263). What follows is a detailed refutation of Harvey's account of the operation of the heart. Descartes is careful to point out that he had reached his own view about circulation before having read Harvey, just as he had made the advances in mathematics without having read François Viète (AT 3. 187); his own experiments on animals to establish the mode of the heart's operation are recounted in a letter to Vopiscus Plempius (1601–71) dated 15 February 1638 (AT 1. 526–7).

44 *various humours*: *humeurs*: this word is usually reserved for the four humours which go to make up the temperament or complexion (blood, choler, yellow bile, and black bile, corresponding to sanguine, choleric, phlegmatic, and melancholic); but Descartes uses it here and in the

Treatise on Man (AT 11. 127–8) to designate the transformations of blood into saliva, urine, sweat, and other excreta.

45 *animal spirits*: the name of one of the three Galenic spirits: natural, which constitutes the powers of appetite, change, and generation; vital, which animates the heart; animal, the source of rational thought and its lesser equivalent, the *vis aestimativa*, in animals; in Descartes's mechanistic account, animal spirits are simply the smallest particles of the blood, and have no vital functions.

subtle: *subtil*: composed of very small, fast-moving particles.

intended to publish: viz. *Le Monde*; *L'Homme*, on which see Introduction, pp. xxiii–xxviii.

to be the sensus communis: see Introduction, p. lvi.

46 ... *real human beings*: the theory that animals are no more than machines led to some disagreeable results: Descartes's disciple, the theologian Nicolas Malebranche, is said to have kicked a pregnant dog, and then to have chastized such critics as Jean de La Fontaine, the French writer of animal fables, for expending their emotions over an unfeeling machine that moves and makes noises depending merely on how and where it is stimulated, rather than concerning themselves with human misery.

47 ... *they have none at all*: Descartes may well have in mind the long (polemical) defence of the reasoning powers of animals in Montaigne's 'Apologie de Raymond Sebond' (*Essais*, 2. 12).

48 *like a pilot in his ship*: the analogy is taken from Aristotle, *De anima*, 2. 1, 413a 8–9.

feelings: *sentiments*: this term can denote both sensations and beliefs.

49 *to conclude that it is immortal*: on the currency of the debate about the immortality of the soul, see Introduction, pp. lvii–lviii. Gilson, *Discours*, 436–8, points out that Descartes is only able to claim that the soul is possibly immortal, since its continuing existence would depend entirely on God.

50 *published ... by someone else*: a reference to Galileo, *Dialogue Concerning the Two Chief World Systems* (1632), condemned by the Congregation of the Holy Office, in 1633; see Introduction, pp. xxxiii–xxxiv.

the business: *métier*: Descartes's sense of his aristocratic status is apparent here: see Introduction, p. viii.

51 *as many reformers as there are people*: this is the negative version of the statement which opens the *Discourse*: see above, note to p. 5, 'Good sense'.

the speculative philosophy ... possessors of nature: the speculative philosophy of the schools is of course Aristotelianism; Descartes's hope that men might become the 'masters and possessors of nature' is consonant with the programme set out by Francis Bacon in the *Instauratio magna* and the *Novum organum* (2. 52)

on the temperament: *tempérament*: the combination of the four humours which is idiosyncratic to each individual.

52 *be free of innumerable illnesses . . . old age . . . provided us*: the prolongation of life was one of the ambitions of alchemy.

experiments: *expériences*: on this term, see above, note to p. 26, 'many experiences'.

specific: *particulières*: peculiar to a set of circumstances.

53 *Forms or Species*: Descartes capitalizes these two words to mark his use of them in their scholastic meaning.

56 *the disputations . . . in the schools*: on Descartes's strong reservations about disputations, see the preface to the French edition of the *Principes*, AT 9B. 7–8.

58 *learning it . . . for themselves*: having talked about divulging his physics, Descartes now hides it: his motive appears to be to prevent others from claiming that they are continuing his work. The gesture is similar to his practice of setting very difficult or incomplete geometrical problems for his correspondents, on which see Introduction, pp. xx, lxii–lxiii.

59 *. . . would never do*: a reference to the practice of alchemists: see Introduction, p. xiii.

60 *three years ago*: i.e. in 1634. Descartes is probably referring to his 'open' letter of April 1634, on which see Introduction, p. xxxvi.

some individual essays: *Dioptrics*; *Meteorology*; *Geometry*, on which see Introduction, pp. lx–lxiii.

61 *. . . 'suppositions' . . . to prove them*: it is not clear how this relates to the claim to have worked out everything from first principles.

if the last are proven by the first . . . their effects: there is a reference here to the logical procedure known as *regressus* (the passage from a demonstration from effect to one from causes), on which see Nicholas Jardine, 'The Epistemology of the Sciences', in *The Cambridge History of Renaissance Philosophy*, ed. Charles B. Schmitt, Quentin Skinner, and Eckhard Kessler (Cambridge, 1988), 686–93, and Introduction, pp. lxi–lxii.

the fallacy that logicians call a 'circle': Descartes is referring to the fallacy known as the *petitio principii* (where the conclusion is presupposed in the premiss). On circularity of argument, see above, note to p. 33, 'comes from Him', and Introduction, pp. lv–lvi.

as empirical evidence: *expérience*: on this term, see above, note to p. 26, 'many experiences'.

62 *no apology for their being new*: in an age in which reverence for ancient

learning underpinned much 'scientific' activity, this is a bold statement of independence.

62 . . . *only by the books of the ancients*: there is an echo here of a phrase used to justify 'the liberty of philosophizing' ('nullius addictus in verba magistri'): see Introduction, p. xxviii.

63 *useful to some by harming others*: Gilson, *Discours*, 477, says that Descartes has military engineering in mind here.

INDEX

Note: the footnotes to the Introduction are indexed by note number, thus xxxi n.22; the Explanatory Notes are indexed by page number, thus 75n.